WORLD'S END FOR SIR OSWALD

WORLD'S END FOR SIR OSWALD

Portraits of Working-Class Life in Pre-War London

Alf Goldberg

Edited by Barry McLoughlin

The Book Guild Ltd
Sussex, England

The Book Guild Ltd.
25 High Street,
Lewes, Sussex

First published 1999
© Alf Goldberg, 1999

Set in Times
Typesetting by
SetSystems Ltd, Saffron Walden, Essex

Printed in Great Britain by
Bookcraft (Bath) Ltd, Avon

A catalogue record for this book is
available from the British Library

ISBN 1 85776 485 4

CONTENTS

The author wishes to thank David Walker for his help in providing photographs of the World's End from the collection at Chelsea Library.

FOREWORD

by Tony Benn

ALF Goldberg has written a really important book about his own life in pre-war London and the interplay between the community where he lived and the Fascists under Sir Oswald Mosley.

Not only is it beautifully written with rare insights into the circumstances of the time, but 60 years later, at a moment when world capitalism is back in crisis and despair is creeping back, we would do well to be reminded of the conditions which led to the rise of the Right, with its tragic consequences for individuals and the inevitable drift into war.

TONY BENN MP,
House of Commons,
London.

CONVERSION TABLE

All sums quoted are in 'old' – pre-decimalisation – money, comprising pounds (£), shillings (s) and pence (d). There were 12 pence in a shilling and 20 shillings in one pound.

One new penny is, therefore, equivalent to 2.4 old pence – 2.4d. A farthing was a quarter of an old penny and a halfpenny ('ha'penny') was 0.5d.

Other useful equivalents:

Twopence (2d, 'tuppence')	0.8p approx.
Sixpence (6d, a 'tanner')	2.5p
One shilling (12d, a 'bob')	5p
Two shillings ('two bob', a florin)	10p
2s/6d (a half-crown)	12.5p
Five shillings ('five bob', a crown)	25p
Ten shillings ('ten bob')	50p
Fifteen shillings ('15 bob')	75p
One pound (£1/-)	£1.00p
One guinea (21 shillings)	£1.05p

8

1

WHEN THE KING'S ROAD SWUNG
TO THE RIGHT

I never met Sir Oswald Mosley – an omission which, I am sure, neither he nor I regretted. Our paths crossed many times, however, and our lives were to become, for a short time, intimately intertwined. He, of course, would have been unaware of my presence anyway. As the charismatic but impetuous and demagogic leader of the British Union of Fascists in the 1930s, he would have had no reason to acknowledge a left-wing Jewish boy from the district of west London known as the 'World's End'. But I was fortunate to receive what I believe was a unique insight into his activities, and I like to think that I made some small contribution to his nemesis.

There were certain similarities between us: we had both boxed (he for Winchester from 12 years old – the age at which I became West London schoolboys' champion); and we were both fighters in other ways, holding passionately committed views on politics. But he was nearing 40 – twice my age at the time – and had swung violently to the right. He was one of that peculiar breed of politician of whom it could be said they might just as easily have become leader of the Labour Party as of the Conservative Party. In the event, he was to become neither, and was to be consigned to the wilderness that exists beyond Westminster politics.

In 1918 he had entered Parliament as Conservative MP for Harrow at the age of 22 – the youngest in the intake that followed the General Election held a month after the Armistice on 11 November. He fought the election on an unorthodox Tory programme that combined patriotism and promotion of Empire with public ownership and housing grants – what he would later call 'socialistic imperialism'. Impatient with the Tories, however, he subsequently sat as an Independent and eventually crossed the floor to become Labour MP for Smethwick in 1926. Three years later he was appointed Chancellor of the Duchy of Lancaster in Ramsay MacDonald's Labour Government, as the minister with special responsibility for tackling the unemployment crisis. (He had hoped for a more senior position – possibly even Foreign Secretary – and was disappointed that the post was outside the Cabinet.) He honed his rhetorical skills with stirring speeches to successive party conferences; unfortunately, though, he was subsequently to use these skills in the most provocative form of mob-oratory.

He quit the Government the following year and became the focus of a caucus of mainly young Labour left-wingers, such as Aneurin Bevan, disillusioned by the apparent lack of Government action to tackle appalling levels of unemployment in the wake of the First World War and the deep economic depression. Bevan, ironically a fierce and uncompromising opponent of fascism, was one of the principal authors of the 'Mosley Memorandum' in 1930; its main proposal was for an emergency Cabinet of no more than five members 'invested with power to carry through the emergency policy' to help the 2.5 million unemployed. At this time, Mosley was advocating Keynesian solutions to the crisis, urging the regeneration of spending power in the economy by vast public works projects. The manifesto's supporters came to be known as the 'New Labour' Group, 60 years before the phrase was annexed by a decidedly different sort of Labour politician.

In March 1931 Mosley set up the ill-fated and short-lived New Party, and was expelled by Labour for 'gross disloyalty'. He lost his seat in the General Election in October of that year. Disenchanted with what seemed to him the timidity of mainstream politics – and convinced of his own destiny as a great leader – he formed the BUF in 1932. He was unrecognisable as the maverick who had railed against the evils of world capitalism during the 1920s. Now, communism was the great enemy.

Mosley's movement put the emphasis on discipline, fighting readiness and love of order; his adoption of black fencing-jackets for his followers (as well as a champion boxer, he had also been a formidable fencer at Winchester) was ostensibly to make it easier, in case of trouble, to distinguish between friend and foe. At first, the party's symbol was the old Roman *fasces* – a bundle of bound sticks – but this was later replaced, as he sought to distance himself from continental fascism, by an emblem depicting a bolt of lightning in a circle, which we derisively dismissed as the 'flash in the pan'. In his own speeches and writings, Mosley was careful not to avow anti-semitism openly, and he sometimes specifically repudiated it: his party's first manifesto, in 1932, made no mention of Jews. Indeed, he was even called a 'kosher fascist' by some disaffected extremists, who were concerned that he was demonstrating insufficiently overt anti-semitism. But Mosley must have been well aware that many of his supporters were not as scrupulous as he was in disavowing prejudice against the Jews.

Mosley, who was invariably known as 'Tom' to his intimates, was the scion of minor aristocracy, the heir to a baronetcy and estate in rural Staffordshire. His father, also Oswald, was a gambler and rake, and emotionally aloof, providing wealth but little love. Unlike the World's Enders, the upper-classes and *haute bourgeosie* in Edwardian England, when Mosley was brought up, found it hard to show affection to their families. Mosley once remarked that it was held to be easier in that era to show emotion to animals – such as the hunting horses and dogs that dominated their lives – than to other people. By contrast, my own father, from Jewish immigrant stock, gave me a loving, if somewhat impecunious, start in life. Unlike Mosley, too, I have spent all my life on the left – not just a few years, as he did – and events in 1930s London only helped reinforce and buttress my beliefs. Indeed, my entire political outlook was moulded by the social conditions in which I was raised in a tough, yet curiously compassionate, corner of the capital.

11

Like many young Yiddishers, I was brought up in an area where extreme poverty and ostentatious wealth enjoyed an incongruous co-existence, in an improbable cocktail of deprivation, bohemia and conspicuous consumption. Both these environments were the fascists' natural *milieu*: the tenements provided the ground troops and the West End café society the money and political muscle. As a motor mechanic to the moneyed classes of pre-war London, I was perfectly positioned to witness the comings and goings of the Mosley set and its high-society fascist fellow-travellers. I believe this heterogeneous upbringing gave me an unparalleled opportunity to observe the social divisions that formed such a fertile breeding ground for the far right in the febrile atmosphere of 1930s London. It also allowed me to observe, at close quarters, the rise and fall of one of the most powerful – but woefully mistaken – orators of the pre-war era.

The World's End area of Chelsea seems a world away from my current home in Staining, a picturesque and deceptively somnolent village three miles outside solidly proletarian Blackpool, dominated by an eighteenth-century windmill.[1] In contrast to Staining, the King's Road – running the length of Chelsea, from Stanley Bridge at the western boundary to salubrious Sloane Square in the east – was the bustling backbone of the royal borough. Throughout the 1920s and into the 1930s, it was just as 'swinging' as it was to become, once again, three decades later. In 1979 the late Sir John Betjeman, a lifelong Londoner, remarked on how little Chelsea had changed in the previous 50 years. In the Chelsea Arts Club, he wrote in an article in *Books and Bookmen*, there was a painting by Napier Hemy of part of the river bank, 'which conveys that Chelsea is a village on the Thames and not part of London'.

A journey down the King's Road took the traveller from the abject poverty of the World's End area, with its spider's-web of flat-crammed, mean little streets stretching down to the embankment of the Thames, to the affluence of Sloane Square. One of the meanest was a *cul-de-sac* called Slaidburn Street. Never in my childhood experience had I known a member of the local constabulary to venture alone into its murky depths after nightfall. It differed starkly from salubrious Sloane Square, which, with its Royal Court Theatre and Hotel, was the gateway to the ostentatious wealth of Eaton Square and Belgravia.

Despite the juxtaposition of prosperity and poverty, there was no apparent demarcation of lifestyles: the King's Road was genuinely cosmopolitan – from the members of the royal family who could sometimes be spotted slipping discreetly from their Daimlers into an an antiques shop, and the 'haves' who shopped at the Peter Jones department store, to the Bohemians who frequented their favourite cafés or the 'Six Bells'. Each pub – and there were many – attracted and catered for its own community, whether the so-called 'golden dustmen' (see Chapter Nine) or the artistic set. It was particularly in the evenings that the King's Road would 'swing'. Its attractions included its small candle-lit restaurants, its dance academies, and the events at the Victorian Town Hall and the inimitable Chelsea Palace. Here, everyone who was anyone in the entertainment and theatre world would appear: artistes as diverse as the Rochdale-born 'black-face' singer G.H. Elliott – known as 'The Chocolate-Coloured Coon' (these were the days before political correctness!) – and the celebrated ballet dancer Anton Dolin. Once I even paid ninepence to see Louis Armstrong, before he became famous, play to an almost empty house.

Apart from Wren's stately Royal Hospital, the Palace and some of its churches, Chelsea had relatively few outstanding examples of architecture, but its strength was in its people: there were many local characters who stood as tall as any grand neo-Gothic edifice. The area remains a social melting-pot even today, with the Cremorne Estate accommodating everyone from pensioners and families to professional people and media types.

In those pre-war days, the World's End comprised about an acre of former farmland around the eponymous pub in the King's Road. Though there was a certain grim, apocalyptic finality about its name – which was never an official postal

13

address – there had, in fact, been several World's Ends. The name first appears in the middle of the seventeenth century on a handful of inns around the capital, including the tavern at Chelsea. This 'World's End' was known to King Charles II.

Geographically, the area was relatively easily defined, though its boundaries were fluid and the subject of conjecture. Beginning at the double-bend in the King's Road near Milman's Street, by the old Chelsea Police Station, the World's End was sandwiched between this northern boundary and up-market Cheyne Walk on the Embankment. The south-western boundary stretched beyond Edith Grove to Lots Road and Chelsea Creek.

The pub was the hub of the busy working-class neighbourhood, which, despite its stifling poverty, still managed at times to exhibit a certain gaiety. At least it was never dull. There was a rough-and-ready neighbourliness which occasionally flared up into passionate protest: free speech was another prized part of the life of the community. There were riots in the 1880s and again in the early 1900s. But there was a deep and irremovable bond of comradeship between its residents, a togetherness that has survived the post-war redevelopment of the area. This was perhaps best exemplified by the events on the nights of 6 and 7 January 1928, when the wind-lashed Thames burst its banks at high tide and flooded the low-lying houses. Tom Manley, a prominent local Labour Party member, and his wife braved the storm to help co-ordinate the sandbag-laying, tea-brewing, soup-ladling operations, and cross-party political pressure eventually led to a strengthening of the river defences (though John Betjeman later claimed the embanking of the Thames had ruined the area).

At the centre of the World's End was a large traffic island which served as a stopping stage for the two busiest bus routes in London at the time – the Nos. 11 and 22. It also housed a news-stand, two telephone boxes and the parking place for the inevitable coffee kiosk which, complete with canvas awnings, was put into position for business from early evening until the small hours of the morning. There were also two fully-staffed underground urinals – which, like the Windmill Theatre, never

14

closed. Most importantly, however, there was space for a 'speakers' corner', which was regularly used as a venue for meetings held by all the political parties and organisations of that era. It was a constant source of political education, of which my friends and I took full advantage. At election times, we would listen to such notable speakers as the philosopher Bertrand Russell and the former Conservative Foreign Secretary, Sir Samuel Hoare. As far as the latter was concerned, it was the entertainment from the heckling rather than the content of the speech that provided the attraction.

Then, one day in August 1933, King's Road stopped swinging. That was when Sir Oswald Mosley arrived in town. From then on, louts in their black-shirted uniforms began to appear, mingling with the people but visibly out of place. Supported by the lower aristocracy, of which Mosley was himself a member, they seemed to have no limit to their available expenditure. The BUF had expanded so rapidly that it had to move from its HQ in Grosvenor Place to the aptly-named Whitelands in the King's Road, a vacant former private teachers' training college next to the Duke of York's Territorial Army headquarters near Sloane Square. He transformed the imposing building, which was said to be capable of housing 5,000 members (it was badly damaged during the Blitz and later demolished), into a virtual BUF barracks – known by its occupants as 'Black House' and by its opponents as the 'Fascist Fort'. I would regularly walk down the King's Road past the building, and see the two sinister-looking Blackshirts on sentry duty at its entrance – alongside which were posters with such slogans as 'Fascism, King and Empire'. From inside the building I could hear the constant clatter of typewriters as the Union's secretaries committed their Leader's instructions to paper. Printing presses rumbled as they produced thousands of copies of *The Blackshirt*, the movement's first weekly newspaper. Cars screeched into and out of the yard, their occupants emerging with a self-important urgency. The callers included celebrated literary, business and sporting figures.

The place was run on military lines, guarded by a hand-picked BUF 'defence force' – the so-called 'I' squad – with reveille, meal-times and lights-out dictated by the calls of a bugler under the command of Mosley's young Chief of Staff, Ian Dundas. As well as the 'I' squad, Mosley also recruited what amounted to a private army to carry the message beyond Black House: he enlisted any unemployed or homeless mercenary who was willing to exchange his brawn and allegiance for a uniform, food, a roof over his head and the likelihood of violent rough-houses.

Black House remained thus for two years until, in 1935, the BUF moved to smaller offices in Great Smith Street, Westminster, partly for economic reasons and partly because Mosley always favoured a small, tightly-knit vanguard in control of the party rather than a profligate and top-heavy hierarchy. The World's Enders were not sorry to see them go.

Being so close to these historic events at this time brought home to me and my immediate friends, with startling clarity, the awful realisation that evil, in the form of fascism, was real and present, not just something we had read about in Sinclair Lewis's novel *It Can't Happen Here*. Even so, little did we realise that, by then, Nazism was already perpetrating its foul doctrine of racial, religious and political persecution on peoples in other parts of Europe. How could we? At this very time, headlines in newspapers like the London *Evening News* and the *Daily Mail* were screaming: 'Why Everyone Should Become a Blackshirt!' Once, a newspaper even published an article purporting to come from a Jewish East Ender, explaining why it was a good idea for Jews to follow his lead, join the BUF and become Blackshirts!

It was the big newspaper proprietors, the Lords Rothermere and Redesdale, who were largely responsible for this disgraceful state of affairs. Rothermere, who had partnered his fellow press baron, the Canadian-born publisher-politician Lord Beaverbrook, in a campaign for 'Empire Free Trade' in 1929, was attracted to Mosley's emphasis on action rather than words. Rothermere himself contributed articles, which I read with horror, under headlines such as: 'Give the Blackshirts a Helping Hand', 'The Blackshirts Will Stop War' and 'Hurrah for the Blackshirts!' He put his *Mail* group, as well as his

16

highly influential chain of regional newspapers, at the service of Mosley for a while, and, between 1934 and 1936, it seemed as though fascism could take hold (although Nye Bevan was reported as saying: 'Nothing could do more damage to Sir Oswald Mosley's little movement than the sudden adherence of the Rothermere press.')

Lord Redesdale was active on the ruling council of The Link, an openly Nazi front organisation, and made speeches about the supreme ideals of Hitlerism. With other big financiers close to the minor aristocracy in Britain, the two press barons supported Mosley to the hilt. This was not surprising as they were a tight clique, bound in some cases by family ties. In 1920 Mosley had married Lady Cynthia ('Cimmie'), second daughter of the former Foreign Secretary, Viceroy of India and unsuccessful Tory leadership contender, Earl Curzon of Kedleston. But in October 1936, three years after Cimmie's death, he secretly wed the third daughter of Lord and Lady Redesdale, the society beauty Diana Mitford, after her divorce in 1933 from the novelist Bryan Guinness (later Lord Moyne). Her sister, Unity, was a close friend of Adolf Hitler's: in his *Sunday Pictorial* of 24 April 1938, Redesdale wrote of rumours of his daughter's engagement to Hitler: 'The Führer lives only for his country and has no time for marriage.' In September 1939, after the outbreak of war, Unity Mitford shot herself in the head in Munich in a failed suicide attempt. Hitler visited her three times in a clinic in Munich and later arranged for her to be moved to Berne in neutral Switzerland so that she could be collected by her family and returned to Britain; he personally paid for all the moving and storing of her furniture until 1945.

During those early days in 1933, we were able at close range to watch Mosley's movement expand with frightening speed. This taught us some lessons, among which was the fact that Sinclair Lewis was right in his American novel to stress that fascism can so quickly turn from a spark into an inferno if good men do nothing. Not that Mosley's movement did become a raging fire. Although he had the necessary ingredient of financial backing, 'good men' – in the person of the

17

local working class – refused to 'do nothing': they fought back and he was eventually defeated.

Soon after Mosley had converted Whitelands College into a barracks, large armour-protected vans began to appear from the premises nightly, *en route* to town halls and other political speaking venues across London and towns and cities elsewhere. Generally, the routine was that the vehicles would arrive at a venue in the evening. They would then be ringed four or five deep by the Blackshirts, like uniformed zombies. The loudspeaker system would be rigged up and Mosley would appear on the top of a van in the middle, in the glare of floodlights. That he was a talented orator, with a sense of theatre, could not be disputed; but nor could the fact that he was an evil racist.

On most occasions, these meetings would end with fights and other disturbances, generally between the police and the anti-fascists, with the Blackshirts having made their getaway in the vans. Occasionally, extremely serious disturbances would take place. This was particularly so when the infamous BUF rally was held at Olympia, London, on 7 June 1934, at the peak of the movement's popularity. This was the one venue in the capital bigger than the Royal Albert Hall, where the fascists had held an unusually orderly rally two months earlier. On the day, anti-fascist marches converged on Olympia from five different parts of the city. That morning the *Daily Worker* had published a map of how to get there and proclaimed: 'All roads lead to Olympia tonight!' Anti-fascist demonstrators managed to infiltrate the meeting, occupying a sizeable minority of the 13,000 one-shilling seats available. I was not at the rally but I received eye-witness accounts later. As Mosley strode beneath the glare of the arc lights on to the platform, flanked by four blond Blackshirts, the interruptions had begun immediately: opponents shouted slogans such as 'fascism means murder'. Mosley warned the demonstrators to stop or be thrown out. They refused, and stewards descended on them. Impartial observers like the MP Geoffrey Lloyd spoke of half a dozen Blackshirts carrying a protester out while other fascists punched and kicked him. Three Tory MPs wrote in a letter published in *The Times* the following day that the Blackshirts had inflicted 'wholly unnecessary violence' on protesters. Mosley, meanwhile, had stood defiant on the platform, hands on hips. Many other people were injured, with some reportedly being thrown from balconies. The Olympia rally marked a watershed for the BUF: until then, its meetings had attracted some more moderate, conservatively-minded people, unhappy at the state's apparent inertia, as well as the troublemakers and the terminally disaffected. In July Lord Rothermere withdrew his newspapers' support: it had lasted barely six months. For Mosley and his fascists, the rally was what would now be described as a public relations disaster, though, in those days, the concept of politics as PR was unheard of.

Mosley was always well-protected and generally escaped unscathed, though he was struck in the face by a stone in Southampton and, when he ventured north to Liverpool, he was hit on the head by a broken brick thrown at his cavalcade by a protester. He was in hospital for a week recovering from an operation for a wound on his skull. From the first appearance of his men in Chelsea, too, he faced outright opposition from me and my friends in the neighbourhood of the World's End. At times, this opposition was effective, albeit in a small way. But it could also be dangerous for us, as on the occasion when Mosley's racist abuse proved too much for one of our party after we had infiltrated a BUF rally in the Chelsea Town Hall and were seated in the gallery of the auditorium. (With its granite base and elegant Ionic porticos, the Town Hall was an unlikely venue for such a rabble-rousing event.) My friend couldn't resist the temptation to heckle. Considering that we were sitting towards the front of the gallery, and the only two exits were small doors at the rear, reached by aisles heavily protected by Blackshirts, this was probably not the wisest course of action. At the end of the meeting, we all managed to reach the safety of the cold pavement in the King's Road – but not before most of us had felt just how hard was each of the stone steps leading from the gallery to the street!

During this time I was employed as an improver motor

mechanic at Moon's garage, an imposing five-storey building in Buckingham Palace Road, near Victoria Station on the edge of the West End. Working there, I was ideally placed to observe the actions of Mosley's organisation much more closely than many of his other opponents. (It was, of course, pure coincidence that many problems befell the BUF transport fleet during the time I worked at the garage!) The workshop was on the top floor, while the other four storeys were used for contract parking. Access to the floors was by two large car-lifts; turntables on each floor facilitated the parking of the vehicles. Because of its position, many famous names and wealthy people had contracts to house their cars at the garage, and charges were accordingly prohibitive for the majority of motorists. What more could you expect if you wanted to park your car alongside Max Miller's or Barbara Hutton's?

The cost, however, was no deterrent to Oswald Mosley. He stabled several vehicles there, from small sports cars to limousines. This gave me the opportunity to observe some of his party's internal transport arrangements. Periodically, I used to work a late shift in the top-floor workshop, which involved attending breakdowns during the evening, mostly at the West End hotels and in the theatre district around Shaftesbury Avenue. It was at these times that I would see Mosley or other members of the BUF hierarchy arrive, change to a suitable limousine and depart for Croydon Airport, which was then the main London aerodrome for the Continent. On occasions, they would return later in the evening with men who were obviously German officers whom they had collected from Croydon. The Nazi visitors and their hosts would then transfer to smaller cars and proceed to destinations best known to themselves. It occurred to me later, when Mosley and his clique had long since been detained and interned, that one of the destinations for the German visitors was likely to have been Brocket Hall at Welwyn in Hertfordshire. This was the former home of Lord Brocket, the industrial magnate and admirer of Hitler, who had also been interned at the start of the war. In 1945 I was still in the RAF. I collected my wife, Dolly, and new-born daughter, Lorraine – our second child (we already had a son, Alfie Jnr) – from the handsome mansion, which had been commandeered as a maternity hospital for London mothers throughout the Blitz. The change-over must have been rapid as the oil paintings of Nazi leaders still adorned the walls. Dolly had the dubious honour of von Ribbentrop gazing down upon her during her confinement![2] The BUF sought to style itself as a more home-grown product than German or Italian fascism – and Mosley disdained some of the policies of Hitler and Mussolini – but my observations confirmed that the influence of its continental counterparts was greater than the party liked to pretend.

At Moon's we dealt only with Mosley's more conventional vehicles: I suspect that he had his five armoured vans serviced in-house or at a back-street garage rather than at a reputable establishment. Stored in the transport yard at Black House, they had protective metal plating at the sides and wire mesh over the windows, and were used to transport members of the 'I' squad to meetings and rallies. The BUF leadership conceded that they were, in principle, the same as the notorious vehicles used at the time by gangsters in the United States, but pointed out – reassuringly – that 'the design is different'.

While working at Moon's, I remember one incident which, although at the time I treated seriously, I have recalled with amusement in later years. One morning I was approached by the works manager and instructed to test the ability of a prospective new driver for the parts collection van. I was to accompany him on the morning collection from the main distributor depots which were largely located around the London suburbs. We set off amicably, at least as far as I was concerned. I began to realise before we had reached our first call, however, that somehow I was not attracted by his personality. At first, this must have been an instinctive reaction, but it was completely vindicated later when we were about to return to the works. The conversation turned to politics, and he told me not only of his political leanings but also invited me to join his party – the British Union of Fascists! He could not have been aware that I had a good old Yiddish surname. I solved the problem by pushing him out of the cab and returning to the garage alone. Afterwards I did have the additional difficulty of explaining to the manager that we had had an altercation, and that he would be walking back. He never did get the job.

Despite courageous oppposition from anti-fascists nationally and locally, Mosley's influence continued to grow alarmingly. By 1935 he could boast of having a membership of 20,000, and he still enjoyed the support of some of his media millionaire allies. During this time in Chelsea, my friends and I continued to arrange reception committees wherever the fascists met locally, and sometimes further afield. These meetings would take place at all the recognised public open-air speaking venues, such as in World's End itself, Putney Towpath, Lincoln's Inn Fields, and, of course, Speakers' Corner in Hyde Park.

As his movement grew stronger, Mosley became more brazen. In the autumn of 1936, however, he made his great mistake of planning to march right through the East End of London. The attempted march eastward along Cable Street was to be the greatest provocation that British Jewry had ever witnessed, and Mosley's most catastrophic error. The confrontation that day is now known universally as the 'Battle of Cable Street' and recognised by historians as the beginning of the end of the Mosley era.

Jews made up a large part of the East End's diverse population. In an article in *The Spectator* of July 1936 – less than three months before the march – George Lansbury, the veteran East End MP who had resigned as Labour Party leader the previous year, wrote:

The coming of the 'Blackshirts', with their terrible doctrine of hatred of Jews as Jews, has aroused great indignation among all kinds of people ... We view with shame and disgust the conduct of those who come from other parts of London and carry on propaganda of hatred, provocation and persecution against these our fellow citizens, whose only crime is that they are the children of their parents.

22

In a statement that could equally apply today to the tens of thousands of people of Asian ethnic origin in the East End, he added:

Most of them are as English as we are. There is a large proportion who are naturalised, but many Jews are just as much English by birth as are Methodists, Anglicans or Roman Catholics. This wave of persecution would be stupid if it were not accompanied by what amounts to terrorism.

Some 150,000 Jews lived in the East End boroughs, slightly less than a third of the total population. The Jewish population had reached its peak during the 30 years up to the start of the First World War, when thousands of Yiddish-speaking Eastern European Jews emigrated to Britain to escape persecution. Between the wars the population slowly declined as, growing more prosperous, many of them moved out to north London. The Blitz and wartime evacuation hastened this shift. The Asians who largely replaced them are just the latest in successive waves of incomers who have made the East End such a rich and diverse cultural melting-pot – from French Huguenots to Irish Catholics. In the 1960s this immigration from the 'new Commonwealth' saw the establishment of a large Bengali community in the area around Brick Lane in Spitalfields.[3]

The Blackshirts would march through market-places in which Jews were trading; they would jostle the men and women behind the stalls and use foul language in an attempt to provoke them into a disturbance. Sometimes they succeeded, but, when the police arrived, the Mosleyites had usually fled. They scrawled obscene messages on the pavements outside Jewish-owned shops, and the Labour-controlled council in Poplar had to pass a by-law prohibiting the chalking of defamatory statements on footpaths. At open-air meetings, a force of 'chuckers-out' would be employed to manhandle hecklers in the most brutal manner imaginable. Demands for the banning of the drilling and marching of organised groups of men were gathering pace.

Mosley had announced in June 1936 that the fascist effort would now be concentrated on east London. In that month he headed a march to Victoria Park, Bow, where he addressed a crowd estimated at anything from 5,000 to 100,000. For the march Mosley and his high command had worn a totally different sort of uniform, complete with jackboots and breeches: it had disturbingly Nazi overtones. For two months, the Leader was out of action as he recovered from appendicitis and holidayed in Italy. When he returned to the political front line, he announced plans for the biggest demonstration so far. Like Olympia two years earlier, however, it was to be a propaganda catastrophe for Mosley. His two biggest blunders at Cable Street were to underestimate the East Enders' capacity for resistance and, more simply, to pick the wrong day. He chose a Sunday, 4 October. This, of course, was a day when most of the ordinary people of the area were not at work, which was neither good timing nor good tactics. As with the Olympia rally, the march received huge advance publicity in the anti-fascist press, and as the Spanish Civil War had just broken out, the protesters adopted the rallying-cry of the Republicans: 'They shall not pass.'

With typical provocativeness, Mosley had chosen to lead his fascist march through the areas in which the Jewish population was most densely congregated, from Tower Hill through Shoreditch, Limehouse, Bow and Bethnal Green to Victoria Park. Residents of the East End had been advised to stay indoors. Abandoning any pretence of not being anti-semitic, Mosley warned: 'East London will be asked to choose between us and the parties of Jewry.'

In Chelsea we were, of course, aware of the situation, and dutifully journeyed east that day, determined to make our presence felt in front of the fascists. The nearer we got to the East End, the denser the crowds grew. I cannot remember seeing so many people massed together in a demonstration. At one point I managed to get a glimpse of the heads of the 3,000 fascists who were flanked by protecting policemen, estimated afterwards to number about 7,000. Eventually the whole assembly merged into an amorphous mass of humanity, with no-one sure of what was really happening. Reports later estimated the crowds at some 100,000. Despite the confusion, however, it was obvious that the fascist marchers had been halted and would be going in only one direction, physically and politically – backwards. They were forced back to the Embankment by the police and, from there, for safety's sake, dispersed as quickly as possible.

It was not until the next day that we discovered the real story of what had happened. In the build-up to the march, there had been feverish preparations to oppose it: pavements and walls were daubed with anti-fascist slogans, and by the morning of 4 October first-aid posts had been set up and legal advisers were standing by for anyone who might need them. Thousands of people had packed and blocked the East End streets, overturning vehicles and taking vantage positions at windows and on roofs above the roads. From around midday, skirmishes had begun between police and anti-fascists, and there were periodic baton charges. The police failed in their attempts to keep the route clear. By early afternoon, the fascists had formed themselves into a phalanx, ready to parade along Royal Mint Street, closely guarded by the police. The *Morning Post* reported: 'In every surrounding street, dense crowds were being held back by cordons of mounted and foot police.' When Mosley arrived, flanked by motorcycle outriders and standing to attention in his open-top Bentley, he marched through the ranks of fascists, inspecting them, while demonstrators tried to break through the police cordons. It was clear that the BUF was not going to be able to march past Gardiners Corner on their intended route, so an alternative was found further to the south, passing along Cable Street.

As soon as the demonstrators learned of the change, they poured from Gardiners Corner to Cable Street, on the route towards Limehouse. A massive barricade was built, which was defended fiercely by the anti-fascists. Under a barrage of makeshift missiles from the crowd, the police tried and failed to force their way through the barrier, advancing slowly down Cable Street from its junction with Royal Mint Street and Dock Street; they eventually managed to capture it after a ferocious battle in which truncheons and iron bars were wielded. But it had become obvious to Sir Philip Game, the Commissioner of the Metropolitan Police, that it would be impossible for Mosley to proceed without bloodshed and, indeed, loss of life. Alarmed at the threat to public order, he contacted the Home Secretary, Sir John Simon, and was given permission to order that the march be abandoned. Mosley, who professed to believe in the rule of law, had no alternative but to order his men to turn tail and march back west through the deserted streets of the City towards the river. As the news of the fascists' defeat filtered through to the crowd, we could hear cheering start to erupt as protesters began celebrating their famous victory in the debris-strewn East End streets.

The battle, and the other riots which followed the party's marches and rallies, were so violent that Parliament rapidly passed the Public Order Act, banning the wearing of political uniforms in public – which proved a considerable deterrent to the recruitment of Mosley's mercenaries. The Act also gave the Commissioner special powers to ban marches that were considered likely to provoke a breach of the peace. The battle was significant for another reason: it was the only time in pre-war Europe that enormous numbers of ordinary Jews and Gentiles – not just political activists – had joined forces to stage large-scale physical resistance to fascists.

The Battle of Cable Street has gone down in folkore as a victory by anti-fascists over the BUF, and so it was – but, in fact, the two sides never came into conflict. In reality, it was a fight between anti-fascists and police, who tried to clear a way through for the BUF marchers. As Mosley's son, Nicholas, wrote in the *Sunday Telegraph* in November 1996 on the 100th anniversary of Oswald's birth: '. . . the fascists, on police orders, stood meekly to one side, and eventually, to the jeers of the crowds, turned and went home. This was a far more degrading defeat for the fascists than would have been any outcome of direct confrontation with the enemy.' Technically, I have always been able to say of the Battle of Cable Street: 'I was there.' Actually, however, I saw no more than I did at any other of the many political demonstrations which I have

26

attended over the years. Yet, when people learn I was present at that historic confrontation, it is still difficult to convince them that the extent of the massive opposition dwarfed an individual's perception of events.[4]

From that day, Mosley and his movement began to lose influence. Some of his more militant lieutenants left the fascist fold after what they saw as an ignominious rout. For Mosley, it was to prove the apogee of his ambitions. The events that followed are well-known. Mosley and his wife were arrested in 1940. They were held separately until December 1941, after which they were moved to adjoining cells in Holloway women's prison until their release in November 1943. They were then held under house arrest until Victory in Europe Day in May 1945. After two years out of politics, he returned to the fray in 1947 and the following year formed a new 'Union Movement', though he never regained his former prominence. The influx of Afro-Caribbean immigrants in the 1950s was seen by his supporters as giving new relevance to his policies, but his movement's forays into electoral politics almost invariably ended in humiliation. In 1951 he and Diana went to live in Orsay in France, where he died in 1980 at the age of 84. His political and racist opinions remained unchanged.

Interestingly, an article about my plans to write these memoirs, in the local Blackpool newspaper, the *Evening Gazette*, drew a response from another veteran anti-fascist. In a letter to the paper, Donald Lambert, of Blackpool, wrote of his family's involvement in the '43 Group', set up after the war to infiltrate and sabotage Mosley's meetings. One of its most prominent activists was Vidal Sassoon, who, of course, went on to become an internationally renowned hairdresser.

During that era in Chelsea, from 1933 until the outbreak of war, we learned many lessons and truths as a result of Mosley and his fascist movement. For me, the paramount truths will always remain those articulated by Sinclair Lewis. First, the speed with which the incipient evil of fascism can spread like a breeze-fanned blaze through a tinder-dry forest – becoming an inferno virtually overnight.

27

Then, how some of those who control the capitalist system will support the extreme right if they sense they are in danger of losing their power. Finally, that the only thing required for evil to triumph is for good men – and women – to do nothing. And then it would be too late: It *can* happen here.[5]

NOTES

1 As a Labour councillor on Fylde Borough Council (which includes the true-blue area of Lytham St Annes), I was for several years the sole socialist on the authority. Enjoying the sobriquet 'The Socialist Republic of Staining', the village is an improbable bastion of left-wing politics in a constituency that has always returned Tory MPs with impregnable majorities. The nearest it came to witnessing social disorder was in the summer of 1998 when vandals ripped the sails off two ornamental windmills just hours after the village had finished celebrating its success in the North West in Bloom competition.

2 The interned Lord Brocket was not to be the last member of his family to see the inside of a prison. In the summer of 1998 the third Baron Brocket, who had succeeded to the title in 1967, was released from Springhill Open Prison in Buckinghamshire after serving half of a five-year sentence for his part in a £4.5 million insurance fraud involving his fabulous collection of classic sports cars. Among the motives for the fraud were the financial problems caused by his decision to restore the interior of the hall, which had been divided into apartments, to its original state, so that he could live in a manner befitting an aristocrat. Nor has the German connection been completely severed. According to the *Daily Mail* of 8 August 1998, although he had lost control of the family home as a result of the offence, the 46-year-old peer 'gets a reputed income of £170,000 a year after a family trust leased Brocket Hall to a German company'. (The Mosley set didn't seem to have much luck with their ancestral homes. The fascist leader's Burnaston House mansion in Derbyshire, where Blackshirts were trained, had to be demolished in 1990 when it fell into disrepair. Its 3,000 stone blocks were carefully dismantled and numbered, and in 1998 went up for sale for £1 million to anyone who might care to reassemble them!)

28

3 Just as Jewish immigration prompted anti-semitic disturbances in the 1930s so the arrival of the Asians provoked racial violence in the 1970s and 1980s. In June 1978 white youths rampaged along Brick Lane, attacking Bengalis and smashing windows of houses and cars. Intimidation of the Asian population became commonplace – a tactic used by the Mosleyites half a century earlier.

4 The events of 4 October 1936 are commemorated in a graphic mural on the wall of St George's Town Hall in Cable Street, started in 1978 but not completed until five years later after vandalism by the modern-day successors of the BUF.

5 Sixty years on, my constant, nagging fear is that today's generation will take for granted the freedoms they enjoy, freedoms that fascism would have removed from them at a stroke. I am heartened when I see younger people in my part of Lancashire take up the cudgels against the embryonic fascism that is beginning to re-emerge via the extreme-right parties on the Continent, such as the French National Front. (The sub-Mosleyite British National Party has also made desultory attempts to contest council elections in Blackpool, which were fiercely opposed by local anti-fascists, and the resort has occasionally been used for national and regional assemblies of the BNP and the even more sinister Combat 18 group.) The Channel Four drama-documentary *Mosley*, screened in 1998, did to some extent romanticise the younger 'Tom', but I hope it also demonstrated to today's generation the insidious power of gutter-oratory.

As chair of the Blackpool and Fylde branch of the Co-operative Party – it must not be forgotten that Co-operators were in the forefront of the anti-fascist protests of the 1930s – I organised a well-attended public meeting to mark the end of the European Year Against Racism, Xenophobia and Anti-Semitism in January 1998. The main speaker was our local Labour Euro-MP Mark Hendrick, Britain's first black MEP, who had done much to publicise the European Year. I was encouraged by his opposition to the extreme right and by that of the younger activists who, thanks to magazines such as *Searchlight*, are continuing the work which I and my comrades began as young men in the 1930s. I only hope there are enough of them.

I am also encouraged by the indications of a more tolerant multiculturalism that is developing in the capital, the prime example of which is the Afro-Caribbean community's hugely successful Notting Hill Carnival – Europe's biggest street festival – just a couple of miles from my birthplace (though that, too, has occasionally been marred by violence).

Yet there was an appalling postscript to my anti-racism public meeting less than 24 hours later, which underlined graphically the need for continued vigilance against racism. By a worrying coincidence, the incident took place just a stone's throw from the venue of the meeting, the Blackpool Trades Club. The following afternoon a group of racist supporters of Millwall Football Club rained a torrent of abuse on the black footballer Marvin Bryan during their team's away match against Blackpool at the resort's Bloomfield Road ground. Thankfully, it was an isolated incident, and the player dealt with it with dignity and an unmerited tolerance. To its credit, too, Millwall FC has striven hard to stamp out the racism associated with a minority of its supporters, threatening offenders with life bans; and, a week after the Blackpool game, the club helped launch the South London Football Against Racism Initiative. But the incident was still the sort of spark about which Sinclair Lewis warned us.

2

ALFIE

A vast cast of characters played an integral rôle in the life of the World's End during the 1920 and 1930s when I was growing up there, but some were outstanding and special. Among the latter was Alfie. Never have I known a person who managed to cram so much diverse activity into one lifetime and, it must be recorded, with so little personal material gain. Indeed, when he finally died, his entire wealth amounted to a few crumpled fivers in the pocket of an old jacket hanging over the back of a chair.

Alfie had been born and brought up in a large house in the select part of Chelsea well-removed from the World's End, in the Royal Hospital Road, a continuation of Cheyne Walk. His Jewish father had settled there and started a tailoring and furriers' business and workshop opposite the house after escaping the Russian pogroms at the turn of the century. Being first-generation immigrants, Alfie and his two brothers led lives largely free from strict paternal supervision. This was due to their father having to devote most of his time to the task of survival in a new land where he had to launch not only his own business but also those of the family whom he had brought with him to the 'promised land', including a nephew, nieces and several more relatives. He was successful in this despite suffering a handicap common to many of the Jewish tailors and bakers of the day – he was an inveterate gambler. Alfie once told me that, though his father had always had great difficulty in the pronunciation of his adopted mother tongue and could never master the written word, he had no problems deciphering, daily in the *Sporting Life*, what horse the legendary jockey and six-times Derby winner Steve Donoghue was riding!

31

With this family background, therefore, it was no surprise that when he reached the age of 14, Alfie – who was slight of stature – started work at horse-racing stables in Wiltshire as an apprentice jockey. He didn't reach great heights in this profession but he did succeed, somewhat notoriously, in being recorded in the *Racing Calendar* as having been 'warned off the turf' – at the callow age of 16. That surely should have warranted him a place in the *Guinness Book of Records*, had the publication existed at the time. Alfie always maintained that this extreme measure imposed by the Jockey Club was far above any action warranted by that revered institution. According to Alfie, he had fallen out with the trainer's wife so had decided, while travelling to a Hurst Park race meeting, to part company with the horses *en route* and return home to Chelsea. In those days racehorses were transported solely by rail so, when the train had halted at a main junction station, he took the opportunity to make a quick exit, with the acquiescence of a sympathetic 'head travelling lad'. All the authorities were able to charge him with was stealing the riding habit he was wearing when he went AWOL.

Next he secured an apprenticeship as a painter and decorator with the London Office of Works. This involved him working in many Crown properties, including the royal palaces, such as Buckingham Palace, Marlborough House and the Houses of Parliament. He had a fund of stories about his experiences working in these buildings, the authenticity of which had to be taken on trust. These included a conversation with 'King Teddy', Edward VII – himself a devotee of the turf, as well as being much more politically astute than generally regarded – while painting in a corridor at Buckingham Palace. Then there was the occasion when he fell asleep in a sumptuous royal toilet, fortunately waking up in time to book out at the stipulated hour – and avoiding what could have been an embarrassing inquiry.

To supplement his earnings, he joined the cast of a theatrical company headed by Joe Elvin, the Cockney comedian, and spent the evenings on the stage, appearing in racing-themed scenes on the London music hall circuit. He told many tales of the idiosyncrasies of the great music hall stars of the day, such as the generosity of Marie Lloyd and the careful nature of Harry Lauder. These must have been heady days for a young man, and I have to this day a card advertising an appearance by Joe Elvin and his company at the Gaiety Theatre, where, we have been told, they drank champagne from young actresses' shoes.

At the same time as his stage career was blossoming, he also managed – despite having been 'warned off' the turf – to become involved in several ventures connected with the seamier side of the racing world, ranging from racecourse tipster to street bookmaker. The latter occupation, however, had to be abruptly curtailed when the law became aware of his activities. Apparently he been 'making a book' in a Pimlico pub, the Pineapple, unaware that he was under observation by the local plain-clothes constabulary. When the police learned that he would leave his father's house in Chelsea after the race meetings – on the way to the pub to pay out – they pounced on him one evening before he reached his destination and diverted him to Chelsea Police Station. After charging him, they were puzzled to discover that the contents of his leather case comprised clean napkins and a shirt, but clearly no betting slips. It wasn't until the following day in court that the police realised, too late, their monumental mistake. In their eagerness, they had arrested his older brother, Harry, on his way to Harrods, where he was head waiter in the restaurant, and about to begin his evening shift. When Alfie rose in the witness box to testify on behalf of his brother, the officers realised their blunder and gloomily resigned themselves to the inevitable loss of the case. Not that Alfie's brother was a pillar of rectitude, despite his highly reputable and prestigious occupation. Alfie had once helped strap iron rods to his legs, under his trousers, in the hope that he would be deemed eligible to fight 'Iron' Hague, the British middleweight boxing champion, at the National Sporting Club, only then still to be declared 'too light'. It was not just the court case that curtailed Alfie's career as a bookie, however: the year was 1914 and the stormclouds of war were gathering ominously over Europe.

Soon after the outbreak of the Great War, Alfie joined the army as a sapper in the Royal Engineers, seeing service abroad for most of the four years of the conflict.[1] He managed to meet a girl in London, Emmaline, while he was on leave in the middle of the war – some three years before Oswald Mosley met his first wife – and after they married she went to live with his parents in the big house in the Royal Hospital Road. To be merely involved in one war, however, was too mundane for this mercurially complex character: in 1917 the Russian Revolution shook Europe and Alfie found himself embroiled in its aftermath. Already on the Continent, he was sent to Russia as a member of a British Army contingent formed by Winston Churchill. He was never aware why they were sent. But he did explain to me that the Russians they met more or less patted them on the heads and implied that, if they caused no trouble and kept to the cattletrucks that were their quarters, no harm would come to them. This was the case, apparently, for a few months until the day he received personal orders that he was to be drafted back to Britain for compassionate reasons: his father was seriously ill.

It must have taken a long time in the revolutionary days of 1918 to return from Russia to London, and the journey would have seemed endless to Alfie, who was eager to see his father again. He looked forward to confirming with his father, after travelling through the land of his birth, the wonderful stories he had been told as a child about the vast and seemingly endless expanse of its terrain. He was eager to discuss his experiences, particularly as he had been able to improve on the smattering of the Russian language he had picked up from his father. All this was not to be, however. After eventually arriving back in London, Alfie found the house in Chelsea locked and empty, with no sign of his family. He was to learn later that his father and mother were both dead. When his father died, his grief-stricken mother had been found drowned in the Serpentine in Hyde Park. The house had been sold by his brother, and Alfie's wife and child were left without a home; she had moved to a small flat in one of the countless

34

seamy streets just off the World's End, where they lived for many more years.

During his travels with the army through Turkey and Russia, Alfie had contracted malaria and he was finally discharged from the Royal Engineers with a full pension. The disease caused him much suffering with its intermittent bouts of fever, accompanied on occasions by emotional outbursts. The latter were induced particularly by disagreements with any authority figures whom he might encounter. During these episodes, he would develop great physical strength and, once, it took many of the men in the flats to prevent him throwing the landlady down the stairs. (She had offered him a derisive rent rebate for redecorating the flat.)

Despite its slum surroundings, he kept the inside of their home decorated to the standard of those of the upper-class households in which he worked around Kensington – between long periods in the dole queue and undergoing the indignities of the means test. Despite the continuing effects of his illness, his pension was gradually whittled down over the years, after successive medical examinations by the Ministry, until it was completely stopped. This was the treatment meted out to many ex-servicemen in the same circumstances after the First World War.

It says much for Alfie's character that more than 20 years after his discharge, he re-enlisted in his old regiment at the start of the Second World War, in category 'A1'. At 54, he must have been one of the oldest serving sappers in the army. This didn't prevent him completing all the initial drill on the barrack square and the physical training required of recruits. No-one, apparently, seemed aware of his age – not even, for many months, his fellow soldiers in his company at Derby, where he was stationed.

Eventually, his age came to the notice of the company's office. This followed the inquiries of a sergeant-major who had been inspecting the barrack huts while the men were out on the square. He had come across Alfie sitting on his bed, complete with a pail of tea that he had just fetched from the cookhouse. When the sergeant-major asked why he wasn't on the parade ground with the others, Alfie told him he was really 'getting too old for that lark'. Understandably taking umbrage, the NCO replied brusquely that he himself was over 40 and still not too old to take part in PT. 'How old are you, anyway?' he asked. When Alfie told him, the surprised sergeant-major left abruptly to check the records at the company office. The outcome was that Alfie was ordered to report a few days later for an interview with the Commanding Officer, at which it was discovered that he had, in fact, been in the same company as the CO in the previous war. After that, events took a turn for the better. He was given a couple of stripes and put in charge of the garden and chickens at the private house in which the colonel was billeted away from the camp. He held this enviable position – answerable only to the CO – for several months, until the company was ordered to move to the far north of Scotand. By then, the colonel, who had effectively taken Alfie under his wing – even getting him a council house in Derby so that his wife could move away from the London Blitz – had decided it would be much better for him to stay put and to bring his military career to an honourable end. Alfie agreed and, true to the undeniable ability of the 'old soldiers' network' to arrange matters, he had started work within a month – before his company had even departed north – as a civilian worker in a Rolls-Royce factory. Once again, the change in his career prospects was due in no small part to his CO's influence.

As a civilian worker away from his beloved London, however, Alfie was like a fish out of water; after only a few months, he had left the factory and found a small flat near the World's End, giving up his council house and returning to the London bombing, preferring that he and his wife spent their nights in the dubious comfort of Earls Court Tube station. They both survived the traumas of the war, and the post-war years found Alfie back in his original job as a painter and decorator. It was typical of him that he should rejoin the staff of the Office of Works – the establishment he had left half a century earlier. It amused him greatly that some of the bosses were the same people with whom he had started work as an apprentice all those years ago; unlike him, they had never left. He eventually retired with a small pension and, despite an eventful life that had dealt him his share of trials, tribulation and hardship, he was almost 80 when he died. At times, some money had flowed through his hands, but it had never stuck. He left no inheritance but a lot of friends.

Like Oswald Mosley's father, he bequeathed his first name to his son. He was my friend, and my Dad.

NOTE

1   At the same time Sir Oswald Mosley was an officer in the Royal Flying Corps on the Western Front before serving in the trenches and finally being invalided out of active service in 1916; he spent the last two years of the war at a desk job in Whitehall.

3

PHOENIXES FROM THE ASHBURNHAM DUST

Huddled in the shadow of the Lots Road power station, my school was enveloped in an almost perpetual pall of smoke from the four enormous chimneys that dwarfed all the other buildings in the World's End. These chimneys were magnificently constructed, and successfully defied successive attempts by the might of the Germans – who had built them – to flatten them during the two world wars that followed their construction.

But the school, which was named Ashburnham after an obscure lord (at least he was to us at the time), was not as successful as the chimneys in its defiance of the *Luftwaffe*: one of the German bombers' near-misses on the power station managed to demolish half the building. That was a decade after my academic education had been completed, however, on my reaching the great age of 14.

The power station, with its coal-burning furnaces which drove huge, noisy dynamos, powered the entire London Transport system, including the underground trains and the trams. It dominated the lives of those who lived in the area, with its ever-present clouds of dust-laden smoke and ceaseless noise. Ingrained in my memory, as much as it was in the pores of my skin, is the covering of dust that would collect on our books, should we forget to put them inside our small desks during the welcome two hours of dinner time. I am sure that this dust, through the years, must have settled on a wealth of talent and academic potential, despite the lack of educational facilities and the hard living conditions of the students.

These conditions were really little different from those described in Robert Tressell's *The Ragged Trousered Philanthropists*, to which I was introduced before my late teens. Like my father, Tressell – though of middle-class origins – was a painter and decorator, and his novel about the poverty and exploitative working conditions experienced by his fellow tradesmen has become a socialist classic. It was the first novel to reveal the true reality of the destitution and degradation of working-class life during the reign of my father's most famous 'customer', Edward VII. Tressell – whose real surname was Noonan – wrote the book in his spare time and it was published in 1914, three years after his death from tuberculosis at the age of 40. Edwardian England was supposedly a 'golden age' when everyone knew his or her place, yet the pomp and glitter of the era was built on the deception and subjection of the working class. I had also, of course, read Sinclair Lewis's *It Can't Happen Here* and Upton Sinclair's books, around the same period. So, bearing in mind our school leaving-age, we were not backward educationally, at least as far as our class-consciousness was concerned. This was not due, in my case, to the school curriculum or any enthusiasm on the part of the teaching staff, but more to my good fortune in sharing a desk with Gary, a character with whom I shall deal in Chapter Eleven. He came from a somewhat infamous local socialist family who engaged in some hilarious exploits, and to whose influence I willingly succumbed.

There were two teachers, though, who have never faded from my memory: the headmaster and his deputy. This is because of the respect and understanding they showed us, their flock, whom they could easily have dismissed as a ragged, wretched little crowd. The head, at least, had great hope for his charges as, however bad the weather, he would always remove his hat when addressing us outside the buildings in deference, he once told us, 'to, I am sure, some future famous persons'. While I cannot prove it, I'm sure he was right. Certainly I can verify that many years later some of his former pupils had, at least, succeeded financially, and 'they laid them down with a will'.

His deputy, who had been a stretcher-bearer in the Great War, kept us enthralled with accounts of his traumatic experiences during the conflict. He endeared himself to me for ever one afternoon, while recounting an epic wartime episode, when he became so carried away that he declared: 'If there was one lying dead, there was a bloody hundred.' As the use of the expletive in public in those days was confined to eccentrics like George Bernard Shaw, its uttering during the education of elementary school children, although in this case received gleefully, was certainly unorthodox.

I must also record my great debt to him for having pounded into our minds – albeit rhetorically – the words of so many immortal poets that are to be found in editions of the *Golden Treasury*. Occasionally, the pounding could be literal: he would bound up and down the raised gangways between us repeating in stentorian tones the words of the classic verses, punctuating them with heavy thumps on the desks as he passed, and on occasions not being averse to delivering a thump behind an unfortunate and unsuspecting ear, as he urged us to emulate his robust delivery.

He was particularly successful in endearing to me Thomas Gray's *Elegy*, whose wisdom I have treasured ever since. I have always thought that these noble stanzas, though describing the farm labourer's hidden glory, also personified the World's End proletariat. Although, in those early days, our introduction to the beauty of literature was by means of pedantic rhetoric and rote learning, it certainly succeeded in embedding the words in our memories, allowing for future appreciation. In the immense trove of *Elegy*'s beautiful verse, I consider the following most descriptive of the 'World's End Philanthropists':

> Let not Ambition mock their useful toil,
> Their homely joys, and destiny obscure;
> Nor Grandeur hear with a disdainful smile
> The short and simple annals of the poor.

And how could the old headmaster's sentiments be better articulated than in these lines:

Some village Hampden that with dauntless breast
The little tyrant of his fields withstood,
Some mute, inglorious Milton, here may rest,
Some Cromwell guiltless of his country's blood.

(Although the only 'tyrant of his fields' to be withstood in the unequivocally inner-city surroundings of the World's End would be in a window-box, where even a weed would have been welcomed and nurtured until it was recognised!)

During the early 1930s when I was at the Ashburnham School, the solidly-built, three-storey Victorian structure housed a large hall and eight spacious classrooms on each level; it put to shame most of the prefabricated schools that were to be built in the post-war years. The whole school was more than adequately heated by undergound coke-burning furnaces, connected by large-bore pipes to the many heavy, cast-iron radiators throughout the building. In addition, each classroom had an open coal fireplace surrounded by a heavy steel guard, which proved convenient for the teachers to perch on during the cold weather, ensuring them a pleasantly warm posterior. So, at least while in school during the winter, we pupils were always warm and comfortable, although many of us went home to what were little more than cold and draughty hovels.

On the ground floor was the Infant Department, which catered for the reception-class children aged five to those about to enter the Junior Department at seven. On reaching the juniors, the children were segregated, the boys going up to the first floor and the girls to the top storey. Teachers were also restricted to teaching their own sex, while only women taught in the infants. The latter all appeared to be middle-aged spinsters; though there must have been younger teachers somewhere, they clearly never managed to get past our staff selection committee.

The education system was controlled by the London County Council, and, while naturally having some shortcomings, it did provide an education for children up to the age of 14 which, despite more than 50 years of curriculum reform, has not

41

really been bettered. At the end of term in the juniors, an examination was held in every class, covering all the subjects taught. From these results a comprehensive list was produced, showing how every child had fared and their respective marks, which accorded them a position in the class.

The number of children in a class varied from 30 to 40. In the following term the top pupils would move to a higher class. This would generally result in the children in the lower third of the examination positions staying down to repeat the classwork. In this way, the brighter children moved on while the slower learners stayed to take the subjects again. This system naturally took little account of age and resulted in the bright children moving up the school, leaving some of their age-group behind. As one of the brighter pupils, I was always in the top three class positions, so before I was 12 I found myself in the top class with the near-14s – with nowhere else to go before I left school. I had unexpectedly failed the eleven-plus examination, which would have enabled me to enter Westminster Grammar School. This exam was a psychological disaster for me: not only was it held out of normal school hours – on a Saturday morning – but it had also prevented me from playing football for the school in an important match. Its timing was certainly not conducive to encouraging an eleven-year-old to give of his best in an exam which, although he failed to realise it at the time, would be one of the most important milestones of his lfe.

I had, evidently, received a near-miss mark as I was offered a place at Chelsea Central School, which was classed, at that time, as secondary education as distinct from the elementary type taught at Ashburnham. But I suspect my parents did not encourage me to take advantage of this opportunity because, like most of the other families in the neighbourhood, economics dictated that an early contribution by school-leavers to the family budget was a necessity. I did have other prospects of a good academic education after leaving Ashburnham, but, alas, because of unexpected circumstances, they were not to be.

After reaching the top class early and finishing in first position in the end-of-term examination when I was 13, the curriculum had little to offer me in my final year. My class tutor at this time was a good man and a fine teacher, combining this with a rare respect and liking for us – his little urchins – who definitely reciprocated those feelings. He devoted most of his spare time to out-of-school activities, which included organising the annual English County Schools' sports championships. These were held at nearby Stamford Bridge, home of Chelsea Football Club.

I spent many hours of my school time in that last year running messages all over London and generally assisting him in the organising of the event. His constant appeals for funding for the sports brought him into contact with many chairmen of companies in London and proved extremely fruitful. It was through one of these benefactors, I suspect, that he was able to ask me one morning if I would like to continue my education after leaving Ashburnham by attending a private residential school, with all my fees paid. While I accepted this offer respectfully, I cannot recall feeling very enthusiastic. After all, although at 13 I was streetwise, there was little guidance in my circles about the great importance that further education, after elementary schooling, could have on our lives. Our instincts were directed towards earning wages as quickly as possible to bolster the family budget.

Soon afterwards, however, fate stepped in and decided the issue for me. Three months before I was due to leave school, the whole education system in the Borough of Chelsea was reorganised. Ashburnham became the infant school for the area; the junior boys were moved more than a mile to Park Walk School and the girls to a junior school even further away. In the turmoil of these changes, I lost contact with my teacher and friend. This was entirely my own fault, because on my 14th birthday – through the good offices of Marlborough Street Labour Exchange – I started work at a rainwear wholesalers near Oxford Circus and never went back to school.

43

4

WORK

The reason for my abandoning any attempt to continue my formal education wasn't difficult to fathom: I couldn't resist the lure of earning the regal sum of 12s/6d a week, which would considerably reinforce my finely-balanced finances – and those of my family. The amount was gross, and I still had to pay my return bus fares from the World's End to Oxford Circus and back, six times a week, which proved a problem on this salary.

Initially I solved it by taking a penny half-fare on a No. 22 bus from the World's End to Hyde Park Corner every morning and walking the rest of the way through Hyde Park to Oxford Circus, via Berkeley Square. In this way the return fare cost me only a shilling a week, allowing me to contribute nine shillings to the family exchequer and to retain a half-crown pocket-money. Unfortunately, however, this arrangement proved short-lived due to the alertness of a zealous bus conductor. One evening, after reaching the Chelsea Town Hall stage (the last stop before the World's End on the homeward journey), the walrus-moustached clippie clambered up the stairs and demanded, in anything but hushed tones, a further penny from me. My explanation – that I didn't have another penny and, anyway, was entitled to travel on a child's ticket – was met with the abrupt reprimand, for all my fellow passengers to hear: 'Get off – you need a bloody shave!' I thought this humiliation very unfair, as it was only a couple of weeks after my 14th birthday. I made no further attempt to defraud the General Omnibus Company, however, and resigned myself to paying fourpence a day. Anyway, the incident did not constitute a spectacular launch to my putative career.

One of my duties at the wholesalers in Regent Street, near the BBC headquarters at Broadcasting House, was to carry piles of raincoats, draped over my arms, from the ground floor to the top of the building, via the showroom, for them to be shortened in the workshop. It was while waiting for the lift during the first few days of my employment that an altercation took place between me and another young employee; it resulted in us both dropping our raincoats and resolving our differences in the only way we knew how – with our fists. As the fight took place in the main foyer of the building, the commissionaire, George, became instantly involved. It was at the height of the battle, when George was trying to separate the two combatants on the now-crumpled pile of coats, that the chairman of the company and his *entourage* arrived via the revolving glass doors at the front of the building. They were presented with what was virtually a ringside seat for the *mêlée*. By this time, however, passions were so aroused that not even the chairman's presence was able to bring the conflict to a close; each combatant was intent only on the destruction of his opponent. Eventually, George managed to restore order, albeit at the expense of an uncharacteristically dishevelled uniform, in addition to the crumpled raincoats. Surprisingly, neither I nor my opponent was sacked, but we both received severe reprimands. This could have been due to the fact that the chairman was a self-made Jewish gentleman and possibly identified himself with youngsters resolving their differences in a typical back-street manner, which he understood.

I was not to last more than a couple of months in the job as I lost what residual popularity I had retained with the management when I turned up for work unexpectedly during a Jewish holiday and they realised, despite my good old Yiddish surname, that I was not in fact truly of the Orthodox faith. This was my first lesson in religion and tolerance.

It was later, after a few temporary jobs, that I began to experience an awareness that I was living in a society that was made up of classes, and that I was a member of the 'have-nots'. This feeling was reinforced when, after securing a job with the Great Western Railway as a van guard (working, largely, with some of the GWR's vast stock of delivery horses), I thought I was on the threshold of a railway career, only to find I was dismissed a few days before my 16th birthday. The reason, apparently, was that this great British company could not afford the few extra pennies for the National Insurance stamp it would be liable to pay from that date.

Soon afterwards, though, my career prospects took a turn for the better as, due to an uncle having influence in the vehicle trade, I obtained an apprenticeship in motor engineering at a high-quality engineers in Pimlico. My wages dropped to the monumental amount of fourpence per hour, which amounted to less than 15 shillings a week. I was considered very fortunate, however, as apprenticeships in the still-developing craft of motor engineering, at that time, were scarce and largely reserved for the sons of the better-off.

This became acutely apparent to me from the beginning, because my fellow apprentices were the offspring of professional and business people such as hoteliers, police inspectors and company executives. Indeed, the lad who became my immediate friend had a brother who was an officer in the Grenadier Guards, which was no mean position. These diverse family backgrounds had no influence on our working relationships and, being young men, we developed strong friendships and a collective liking for the trade to which we were apprenticed. Eventually, of course, my friends were able to drive their own cars, which they would gladly share with me, but it was to be a long time before I could pay back their goodwill. At least I took full advantage of this opportunity to acquire a skill in a trade that was to have a great influence on my future.

Some of those who were less fortunate occupied the shady fringes of what would today be described as the 'black economy'. One of these was the occupation of street bookmaker, which, as my father's experiences demonstrated, involved a constant cat-and-mouse game with the local constabulary.

The bookie would always employ a runner as a look-out. The runner would take up a vantage point that would enable him to give a warning shout to allow his employer to vanish in a flash, should any danger in the guise of an undercover detective bear down upon him. Inevitably, there would be a comical chase of the fugitive runner, who rarely eluded capture. The result would eventually be a fine, which would be willingly settled by the boss, whose police record remained unblemished. Some sceptics maintained that the rarity of the bookmakers' appearances in court was due to the occasions when they were seen drinking in their local with someone who had the obvious bearing and demeanour of a police officer.

Sometimes, in the absence of his boss, the runner would take over the task, in the evening after the race meetings had finished, of paying out any fortunate punters. He would seize any opportunity to make a few bob for himself by underpaying those whose arithmetic was awry. For instance, if a punter asked for a quid, he would be told that he was down for only 19s/6d. If the punter protested, it would be queried for a later decision by the bookie himself. On one such occasion, great amusement was caused by a punter asking for five bob and, on being told that he only had 4s/6d to come, exclaiming angrily: 'How the hell can it be 4s/6d when I had a half-crown each way on a non-runner!'

5

UPSTAIRS, DOWNSTAIRS

My early life was characterised by starkly-defined contrasts that occasionally bordered on the bizarre. Brought up in the ghetto-like conditions of the World's End during the Depression, I nevertheless had direct experience – through my mother's occupation – of how the upper classes lived, all of which must have had a confusing effect on my adolescent mind.

We owed our strange double life to the fact that my mother worked for a wealthy family who, for months at a time, lived out of the country. During these long absences my mother, father and I would move into their large house in The Boltons, Kensington, as caretakers.[1] So, as a small boy, although I continued to attend the same school, my home and surroundings alternated between two social and environmental extremes. After months of exposure to the noise and squalor of tenement buildings, and playing in and racing through crowded streeets, I would suddenly find myself transported into the completely contrasting world of tranquil avenues, big houses and large gardens. These spells invariably coincided with the summer school holidays, and I would find myself very lonely, missing my friends and the hubbub of the World's End.

My father, though, had no problems with the change of scenery. In fact, he took full advantage of the opportunities that were presented to him to improve his standard of living. Like most of his fellow building-trade workers, he enjoyed his ale and was not averse to over-indulgence, particularly at the end of the week. On Saturdays – a half-day and also pay day – they would retire to the nearest pub at noon and treat each other to drinks, particularly favouring the foreman (or

48

'coddy'), on whose discretion their precarious employment depended. After closing time, my father would arrive at the big house accompanied by a few of his selected friends, all of whom would be weighed down with bottles of beer. They would make their way up to the second floor and the luxury of a fully-equipped billiards room. This had been designed to cater for the tastes and requirements of the house's affluent owner, so it certainly received no criticism from those members of the proletariat who enjoyed their brief glimpse of a lifestyle dramatically different from the one to which they were accustomed. I wish I could record that the head of the household had made a sudden, unexpected return during one of these sessions, but this never happened. His reactions can only be imagined. But it is certain that his uninvited (at least by him) visitors would have welcomed him as one of their own and offered him a drink with a total absence of embarrassment.

My mother Emmaline, who was a very placid and tolerant woman, never complained: despite the rigours of her hard-working life, complaining was never a part of her nature. She came from a large family in the East London docklands and suffered the fate of most young girls in that area, before the First World War, of being 'placed into service' after leaving school at 14. This meant that she was transferred into the care of an upper-class household in Belgravia in the West End to work as a chambermaid for the extravagant wage of £10 a year. Her hours of work depended on what was happening in the house at the time, which in turn varied largely according to the season of the year. If the family was at home and holding regular dinner parties, for instance, her day could start as early as 6 a.m. and she could work more or less continuously until she went to bed after midnight, when all the entertaining had finished. Life could be easier when the family was abroad or away elsewhere, perhaps on the grouse moors. At all times, however, she was allowed one afternoon off each week, which would enable her to scuttle down to the East End to see her mother and return to the house the same evening. Despite these almost slave-like conditions, she and her counterparts

49

performed their duties competently, loyally and without protest. In fact, some continued in the service of the same family for most of their lives, eventually seeing out their days as an 'old retainer'.

My mother always had an affinity with her employers, most of whom were members of '*Debrett*' society. In later life her relationship with them was one of mutual friendship, based on a sense of reciprocal equality. I found this amusing at times because, for all her contact throughout her life with a different class, she always remained a typical, incongruously Cockney working-class woman who treated aristocrats and artisans alike, with exactly the same respect. At one stage, serving, in effect, as a companion to a titled lady, she would have conversations with a retired general. She evidently held him in some regard as she once confided to me that she 'liked old George. He was a nice old boy.' But I could never begin to imagine what topics they discussed.

Even after her active working life, her former employers would write to her and occasionally visit the dingy basement flat in Chelsea which she refused to leave after she was widowed. I remember when one such lady, after unsuccessfully imploring my mother to visit her at her estate in Surrey, contacted me to try to persuade her to go. I eventually managed to get her to agree, on the condition that I took her there myself, by road. The estate, which was in the Dorking area, proved to be much larger than I had expected, and I had to drive some distance through the grounds before reaching the house. This stood elevated above the gardens, surrounded by a patio that was reached by 20 or more steps. As it was a midsummer's day, the gardens were in bloom and the whole setting was one of beauty and serenity. The lady of the house was sitting on the terrace, obviously awaiting our arrival, and the welcome was warm and genuine.

On the journey down, I had resisted my mother's constant appeals to stop and 'let me have a Guinness' because, as I tried to point out, it would not be etiquette to be received smelling of beer. So the pots of tea that were immediately provided on the terrace, in the heat of the day, were greatly appreciated. Once the preliminaries were over and the tea had been consumed, however, it was evident that my presence was not considered essential to the occasion, as the head gardener was summoned and instructed to accompany me on a tour of the paddocks and other features of the estate. When I returned, about an hour later, these two elderly ladies from totally different backgrounds were still in what seemed to me to be earnest conversation. I was eventually informed that, in the event, I was to return to London alone: my mother had decided to accept an offer to stay for the weekend – a decision which gave me as much pleasure as it obviously did the others concerned.

It was a few years later, when she was in her 80s, that I finally induced her to leave her basement flat and the World's End to live with me in the Fylde Coast area of north-west Lancashire, where my business was now located. She never really seemed to become accustomed to the change of environment or, understandably, to the northern climate, with its fresh and sometimes biting north-westerly winds, and she gradually began to retire into herself. As her hearing was failing, she was provided with a hearing-aid, a device which she rarely switched on, preferring, it seemed, to avoid involvement in the difficulties she was encountering with the unfamiliar, broad local accent. When she eventually needed continuous nursing, she was moved into a nursing home where the communal atmosphere – perhaps more redolent of the close-knit community she had left behind in the World's End – seemed to improve the quality of her life. This was also partly due to the fortuitous presence in the home of a charming old actress who had been an acquaintance of, and had appeared with, the celebrated stage performer Lily Elsie. As my mother had also had connections with this leading lady – long ago, in her 'upstairs, downstairs' days – they had much in common and, doubtless, many memories to share.

She was close to her 90th year when she died, peacefully and, I believe, willingly. She had never become reconciled to leaving the noise of the Lots Road power station generators and the dust, dirt and bustle of the World's End. After her death, I was touched by the genuine regret of the nursing home staff. One young member of the night staff particularly moved me when she told me how much she would miss the entertaining stories the old girl would tell, when the other residents had long retired to their beds, about a London life that had already faded into history.

She and her lifelong partner, whom she survived by a few years, were, along with their contemporaries, characters who had experienced an era that would never be seen again. They lived not only through periods of abject and grinding poverty but also through two world wars. Humankind would never be able to survive another world war or produce again, therefore, people whose characters were similarly moulded by their experiences and the living conditions they had endured.

NOTE

1 The Boltons, one of London's plushest thoroughfares, is now home to a new breed of entrepreneurial aristocrat, with its imposing houses occupied by the likes of the Virgin boss Richard Branson.

6

THE BUG 'OLE

Of all the buildings that were crammed into the World's End, the most important – to me and my friends, at least – was the cinema. This had the name 'Prince of Wales' blazoned across its entrance but, for reasons that are probably self-explanatory, was universally referred to as the 'Bug 'Ole'. In retrospect, the cinema was a phenomenon: not only was it a means of escape – for those whom Tressell two decades earlier had described as 'Ragged Trousered Philanthropists' – from the harsh realities of day-to-day life to the fantasies of the silver screen; but it also achieved this on a shoestring budget.

Its sole owner, who would in later years have been described as an 'entrepreneur', was a first-generation Yiddisher gentleman known to all as 'Morry'. In my memory, no-one ever paid more than eightpence for the best seats in the house, and I well remember the incredulous amusement that was caused when, after a refurbishment of the cinema, a notice appeared on the pay-kiosk that the rear seats would be re-priced at 1s/3d. This was, naturally, totally ignored, and Morry could do nothing about enforcing it.

There was a regular Saturday-afternoon matinée, known as the 'tuppenny rush', which seemed to attract every school-age child in the borough. The eagerness of the young patrons to gain entrance was such that the crowd control expertise shown by Morry and Charlie, his projectionist, would have done credit to stewards on a big-match day at Stamford Bridge; the imperturbable pair struggled valiantly not just to prevent damage to the foyer but to collect the tuppences as well. Once the youngsters were inside the auditorium, their enthusiasm would reach fever-pitch when a light was spotted in the projection room, which was the cue for cries of 'he's up there!', followed by chants of 'show up, show up!'

Hurricane Hutch was their favourite adventurer, and many an apple core was thrown at the screen during the excitement generated by his escapades. Tom Mix, the cowboy, ran him a close second. The seating in the hall amounted to a complete fire hazard, as there was only one side gangway and all the rows ended at a blank wall. In an emergency, it would have been impossible for those at the end of the rows, by the wall, to leave until the rest of the row had been emptied into the single gangway. Fortunately, no emergencies ever occurred, so the audiences were always able (aided by the interminable playing of the pianist at the front) to enjoy the bliss of Gloria Swanson's romances and Harry Lloyd's crazy antics in those old silent films.

Morry, however, had his problems. Paramount among them were the constant worries about covering for his permanent staff in the case of unforeseen or unavoidable absence. The permanent staff numbered two: Charlie and the pianist, Ronnie. His clientele, although used to the many mechanical beakdowns that plagued the early projection rooms, were nevertheless quite prone to showing their impatience in a vociferous manner, if an epic was interrupted for what they deemed a too-lengthy period. Charlie was a genius, not just with his technical knowledge of the projection room apparatus but with all electrical and mechanical equipment. Morry was able to leave all these matters to him and concentrate on his financial and other business problems. Even Charlie, however, had to have some relaxation from the constant operational stress and would, on occasions, leave a part-time projectionist on duty while he had a night out.

It was when Charlie was on one of these outings that a fault developed with the projector during a main feature, and the combined efforts of Morry and the assistant failed to rectify the problem. The audience, predictably, began to voice their disapproval. In desperation, Morry rushed out of the cinema and round to the tenement flat a few hundred yards away where Charlie lived, only to discover that he had already left for an evening's relaxation. As I lived in the next flat and could reasonably be supposed to have some knowledge of his whereabouts, I was immediately commissioned to find him and return him as quickly as possible to the projection room. I set off on my bicycle in the direction of the Fulham Road towards the pub which I knew was a favourite haunt of Charlie's. Although I was only a small lad, I pedalled with determination, knowing that on me depended whether the show went ahead – or whether Morry suffered the traumatic alternative if it did not. Luckily, I succeeded in locating Charlie at my first choice of pub and he, being the good trouper that he was, pedalled furiously back to the cinema with me seated on the rear carrier of the bike. In this case, Charlie was able to use his skill to quell the pandemonium reigning in the cinema with the minimum delay. But I have often wondered what would have happened if I had failed to find him on my bicycle-borne quest.

A few years later, Morry decided to reorganise his financial structure by selling the cinema and buying the sweet stall that stood outside on the kerb. I don't know if this was a financial success, but I'm sure the reduction in his stress-level elongated his lifespan.

It was to Charlie that I owed one of the biggest thrills of my young life. This was when I went into his flat and first viewed the many glittering strands of golden wire that stretched across the living-room ceiling between two wooden broom-handles. Connected to them by more wires, in the middle of the living-room table, I saw, for the first time, that mysterious and – to me, at least – awe-inspiring object: a crystal radio set. When, after much meticulous probing of the crystal, Charlie put the head-phones on my ears and I heard an orchestra playing from some distant part of town, I knew he was the cleverest person in the whole world. This view was not shared, though, by the old uncle with whom he lived: he was all for 'throwing the thing out before there's a bloody explosion'!

Working-class people required remarkable resilience and resourcefulness to survive during this arduous era: if they were unable to sell their labour, they had to abandon the skills of their trade and try to become self-employed entrepreneurs. This was the case with Charlie when the curtain finally closed on the big screen at the Bug 'Ole. He followed in the tracks of his former employer, Morry, by becoming a stallholder with a kerbside pitch in the World's End – selling flowers! Although the business apparently succeeded over the subsequent years, I am sure society was the poorer as a result of the loss of Charlie's undoubted natural expertise in engineering.

7

DUMPY: ALMOST A SAINT

Many of the inhabitants of the World's End spent much of their lives in a semi-nocturnal state as the flats were often wholly, or partly, below street level. Even in the summer, artificial light in the form of a gas-jet or oil lamp was necessary in the basement flats, although in the 1930s the landlords slowly and reluctantly wired them for electricity.

My family's flat was, at least, above ground level, whereas some of my friends on the opposite side of the road were doomed to life in those underground caverns. Among these unfortunates was an unforgettable figure known to all as 'Dumpy'. The derivation of his nickname always remained a mystery; it certainly had nothing to do with his physical appearance, as he was always tall for his age and proportionately well-built. In his early teens he had an angelic face which often proved to be a valuable asset when he most needed some sympathy from a representative of authority with whom he had crossed swords. Unfortunately, this happened frequently because of his innate – and, some might say, inane – passion for daring but dubious exploits.

Because of the prevailing social conditions, it was almost inevitable that he would develop into a rogue, albeit a generous and engaging one. He acquired skills which, coupled with his daring, soon brought him to the attention of the law, although his feats were generally regarded with an amused tolerance in the neighbourhood and he was considered something of a Robin Hood figure. As he was motivated solely by a desire for excitement, any spoils that accrued from his, mostly illegal, activities were invariably distributed freely to all-comers. At one time during the warm summer weather, he developed an aptitude for boarding refrigerated ice-cream lorries by a side central door – while they were in transit. He was then able to unlock an interior door and throw cartons of ice-cream out on to the road before he, too, would leap down. The whole of the street's residents would gleefully share the resulting refreshments.

Probably the most daring of his exploits – certainly the most frightening to me, even in those days – were the pigeon-trapping expeditions that he launched among the steel structures below the roadway of Battersea Bridge. Somehow, he was able to gain access from road level to the metal girders beneath the parapet, and there, in a vertiginous no-man's-land above the Thames, he would trap live pigeons without plunging into the murky depths below. This was just as well: he was a non-swimmer! This pastime was pursued purely to satisfy his craving for excitement, because, like most of his other activities at the time, it was financially profitless. After exhibiting his captives to his street-mates, he would always set the birds free to soar again between the chimney stacks.

Predictably, he was in constant conflict with the local constabulary; it was generally a no-win situation for him, but occasionally he caused the police some embarrassment. I particularly remember an incident when he was apprehended for some misdemeanour by a detective constable. Dumpy succeeded in persuading the unfortunate officer to allow him to visit his mother on the way to Chelsea Police Station. To gain access to his basement flat, you had to go down some narrow, awkward concrete steps from street level, at the bottom of which was the front door. Once inside, you then had to turn directly right and negotiate an unlit passage to reach the rooms of the flat – a manoeuvre that could be difficult for visitors unfamiliar with the layout. Dumpy led the policeman through the door and halfway along the passage, but then quickly doubled back, darted past him and ran through the front door, slamming it shut and leaving the hapless chap floundering in the dark with no hope of a successful pursuit. As he was still a schoolboy, Dumpy was only at large for a short time; he returned home, cold and hungry, the next morning. That episode cost him a few months in a residential reform school and, although they failed to reform his character, they did apparently teach him how to play tennis! This was richly ironic, as the chances of him being able to take part in that game amid the concrete and cobbles of the World's End would have been roughly equivalent to those of playing a round of golf or gaining employment as a shepherd!

As Dumpy grew older, his misdeeds became more serious, and more prone to the attention of the guardians of the law. Instead of pilfering from cars, he broadened his ambitions to the possibility of taking the entire car, even if, initially at least, for the pure adventure of 'joyriding'.

Dumpy had an older brother who attended a grammar school and was his complete opposite: he was introverted and studious, and particularly knowledgeable on the subject of engineering. At an early age the lad was familiar with the theory of the internal combustion engine and, even before leaving school, was able to dismantle and assemble both motor car and motorcycle engines competently.

Tragically, he had suffered a traumatic experience when he was younger and this had affected his personality; he had become withdrawn within himself and spent most of his spare time indoors, reading engineering books, or tinkering with mechanical parts in the back-yard. Unlike other kids, he did not, as it was termed, 'race the streets'. The experience that had such an impact on him had happened when he was about ten. One afternoon he had apparently gone with a friend to fish for sticklebacks in the Thames, off the steps near Battersea Bridge, at high tide. Later that night, when the other boy had failed to return home, his worried parents called at Dumpy's house. His brother was woken up and, after much questioning and prompting, it was established that his friend had fallen into the swollen river and that he had been unable to pull him out.

Hardship and tragedy were no strangers to the back-streets in those days, and emotions sometimes ran high; this case was no exception. But, as always, the sharing of grief and the communal support in adversity helped heal the sorrow. Even so, it is impossible to imagine the anguish in the mind of a small boy who runs home so frightened that he is unable to tell anyone about such a terrifying experience and has to go to bed with the torment torturing his mind.

Fate was not kind to this lad, least of all for giving him a younger brother who was to be instrumental in causing him much trouble. Dumpy, who could be plausible and persuasive, played upon his brother's enthusiasm for all things mechanical, and finally succeeded in inducing him to enlist the help of a couple of his like-minded friends to accompany him on a joyriding jaunt. Despite not sharing Dumpy's carefree character, the boys succumbed to the temptation of being involved with their greatest interest – the world of the motor car – from which, because of their economic circumstances, they would normally have been excluded. But the whole affair ended in catastrophe, and in their being arrested by the police after a car chase. Despite their previously clean records, Dumpy's brother (who had been driving) and his two friends were treated as severely as the instigator by the court, and received terms of Borstal detention. Sadly, this kind of treatment by the courts was common practice in those days. Many youngsters – whose only real crime was being born into this environment – were fated to carry the consequences of a single youthful blunder as a debilitating handicap for the rest of their lives.

It was a decade later, during the Second World War, that I last met Dumpy. As a Flight Sergeant in the RAF, I was on leave in London and was coming out of the Palladium with a fellow NCO: we had just pinched some of Max Miller's latest jokes to include in our camp concert double-act, 'Slasher and Slosher' – I was the former! Suddenly, in the darkness, I felt a hand grip my arm. I turned, and there he stood: tall, handsome and well-dressed in civilian clothes. I felt so disappointed because, if I had ever thought about him, it was to imagine his being dropped behind enemy lines on some moonless night or racing through the clouds in a fighter, having just secured a bar to his latest medal for valour. But there he was, obviously by his appearance too prosperous to be any part of Her Majesty's Forces.

With a glance at the 'crown and three' on my arm, he smiled as he joked: 'You're doing well, Alfie. Do they want any more at your place?' After a short conversation in which he declined an invitation to go for a drink and apologised for being in a hurry, he left in the direction of the West End. As he disappeared into the blackout, I realised that Dumpy was now a fully-fledged professional villain and that, from the touch-lines, I had watched his apprenticeship. I knew also that – as with Charlie the projectionist – it was society, rather than Dumpy, that was ultimately the loser. If it had not been for the environment we were forced to share, his energy, intelligence and gallantry might have been channelled into more productive avenues. It is interesting to speculate about what might have become of Dumpy if he had enjoyed the public school education, privilege and social advantages of Oswald Mosley. They were both quixotic characters, sharing the same sort of drive, dash and flamboyant self-belief; and both had a rebellious streak that would bring them into conflict with authority and eventually see them fall foul of the law, though for contrasting reasons. In another environment, in another life, Dumpy might almost have been a saint.

8

FOR BETTER OR FOR WORSE

World's End weddings between the wars differed from the megalithic matrimonial extravaganzas in the more prosperous parts of the metropolis. First, the lack of money limited the scale of the wedding arrangements. Secondly, as a result, it was more economical to hold the ceremonies, where possible, on bank holidays – such as Easter, Whitsun or even Christmas Day – to coincide with the few days off work and the holiday expenses that already existed. Honeymoons were virtually non-existent as the bride and groom generally had to be back at work within 48 hours of their union.

Billy's wedding was no exception as far as the timing was concerned: Christmas Day in the Church of St Andrew, Park Walk, to be conducted by the local cleric known as 'Old Nuisance', whom we shall meet again in the next chapter. But this wedding did differ considerably in terms of the reception afterwards; it was to be no ordinary 'knees-up' whose success would depend on the number of wooden crates of Watney's Ale available. It certainly was a success, but, thanks to Billy's brother Ron and his friends, the drinks available had more in common with those served at the salubrious receptions held after weddings at the historic and much-restored Chelsea Old Church, further along the Embankment.

Ron had been working for a building firm that was carrying out alterations to a mansion next to Putney Common while the owner was abroad. The work involved repairs in the area of a wine cellar, the copious contents of which they were able to view during a tea-break because, according to Ron, the lock was insecure. As it was December and the weather was chilly, Ron and his mates decided after 'knocking off' work that evening to have a nip to warm them up before their cold homeward journey across the common. After drinking for some time, they reached a stage of contentment at which it was decided to remove some of the champagne to a safer store, where it would not be accessible to any prying building workers who might happen to be around. Having filled a couple of sacks with bottles of the rare vintage, they staggered across the common in high spirits to the terminus from which the No. 22 bus began its journey to Homerton, via the World's End.

Unknown to them, they were to experience agonies of apprehension before they reached their destination. After boarding the bus and climbing to the top deck with their 'luggage', which they dumped in the aisle, they were immediately followed up the stairs by half a dozen uniformed policemen on the way to their beats. In that era, officers would leave the police station in shifts and travel by public transport, each getting off the bus as he reached his 'patch'. As the bus began what seemed to Ron and company an interminable journey, the bottles rattled at every bump on the road, and their palpitations increased proportionately. Luckily for them, there was no prospective Sherlock Holmes among the officers, and not even an 'allo, allo' was heard before they made their respective exits, one by one, along the route. A relieved Ron and his co-conspirators disembarked with their cargo at the World's End and manhandled it to the family home.

Ron was particularly pleased to have arrived safely and unsuspected: not long before, he had been involved in a less fortunate encounter with the law. While he was making his way home on his bicycle after a pleasant evening in the pub, he was stopped by a constable – also on a bike – who asked him why he had no lights, front or rear, on his machine. Ron's reaction to this perfectly reasonable request was to jump astride his cycle and, as he pedalled away furiously, to shout over his shoulder: 'You can't catch me – you're too fat!' But the portly policeman proved him all too wrong by chasing him on his bike for three miles before finally running Ron to earth – literally – and laying across him while they both recovered from exhaustion.

63

Billy and Ron's father was an old regular soldier who, when provided with sufficient lubrication, would wax eloquent about his experiences in what he described as his 'campaigns'. On this occasion, under the influence of such an excellent vintage, his story-telling excelled. In the early hours of the following morning, having talked the whole company into submission long before, he missed his footing as he was trying to negotiate the bend of the staircase. Grabbing the banister, he plunged, with the entire balustrade on top of him, to the bottom of the stairs, where he remained until the next day.

Such was the quantity and potency of the fine wine that Ron and his friends had transferred to safe keeping from its original store that, despite several more convival evenings, they still managed to retain enough to supply Billy's Christmas Day nuptials. This event would long be remembered as unique, even among a group of people whose experiences of receptions, parties and 'knees-ups' was vast. Although some could recall times when immense quantities of Watney's Mild, Taylor Walker's 'Main Line' and even Benskin's 'Colne Spring' had been consumed, never before had all this been complemented by fine champagne.

As the next day was Boxing Day, the bride and groom and the other revellers were spared the impossible ordeal of having to try to rise to get to their workplaces. It was seldom during the year that they were granted two consecutive days free from hard toil. But, on this occasion, they had enjoyed themselves, in their own distinctive way, to the full – even if comparatively briefly. For a couple of days, they had been able to forget the constant struggle and hardship that were the unavoidable lot of all who, in those days, occupied the maze of mean streets that made up the World's End.

The Ashburnham School team that won the Chelsea Schoolboys' Boxing Association Championships in 1928. The author - 'whisker-weight' at 5st 7lb - is at the end of the back row (right). Also pictured are: (back, from left) Gray, Thornett, Byass; (front, from left) Beale, Digweed, Wilde. The photograph was taken at a nearby studio - note the leopard-skin rug in the bottom right-hand corner!

Just a few years before she was 'placed into service', the author's mother, Emmaline, poses in pinafore outside her home in Leyes Road, in the Custom House area of Plaistow in the East End's Docklands, at the start of the 20th century.

Probably the oldest sapper in the British Army, the author's father, Alfie, in his Royal Engineers' uniform during the Second World War. Alfie, who had also served in the Great War, caused some consternation in his company when his age was revealed as 54!

The traffic island was the hub of the World's End in the 1930s and 1940s. The four tall chimneys of Lots Road power station, though somewhat mist-shrouded, still dominated the area. On the island in the centre are the fully-staffed public lavatories and the two telephone boxes. The 'speakers' corner' area was where the three women are pictured in the left foreground. Dartrey Road runs from the left down to the Embankment. On the right are the Home and Colonial stores and the rear of a No. 31 bus in the King's Road. Most of the area is now pedestrianised. *Courtesy: Kensington and Chelsea Libraries and Arts*

The author's home at Westmorland House in Dartrey Road shortly before its demolition. His family lived in the first-floor flat in the foreground, nearest the river. The three children playing on the corner would be about the same age as Alf Goldberg when he lived there. It's unlikely, however, that any of them were asked to emulate the author when he had to climb out of the landing window on to the sill of one of the top-floor flats to let in a neighbour who had forgotten her key!   *Courtesy: Kensington and Chelsea Libraries and Arts*

Much of the life of the World's End revolved around three of the buildings in this picture. The pub has scarcely changed since the 1930s, and still includes many of the original features, including a particularly robust bar. Today, though, the rest of the scene is dramatically different. Next to the pub was the single-storey former 'Bug'Ole' cinema, which was a Salvation Army citadel when this picture was taken in the 1960s. The building has long vanished, as have the flats immediately to the right where the owner, Morry, lived. Blantyre Street runs straight ahead, and the third centrepiece of the community - St John's Mission Hall - is on the right.   *Courtesy: Kensington and Chelsea Libraries and Arts*

The narrow and brooding World's End Passage in the 1960s. The Dickensian former horse-meat shop was at the far end on the left, near the pub and the 'Bug'Ole', where the passage became even narrower. Today the area is occupied by a distinctive new landmark: the local authority-owned multi-storey flats of the World's End Estate; here the names of some of the original streets - including Dartrey Road and Blantyre Street - survive. The flats have panoramic views of the Thames and Cheyne Walk, home of such 19th century luminaries as the Pre-Raphaelite painter and poet Dante Gabriel Rossetti. James McNeil Whistler and J.M.W. Turner were among other artists attracted to the area.
Courtesy: Kensington and Chelsea Libraries and Arts

A Co-operative Party banner forms the backcloth as Alf Goldberg and the former leader of Lancashire County Council, Louise Ellman - now M.P. for Liverpool Riverside - display the National Petition for the NHS at Blackpool Trades Club in the early 1990s.
Courtesy: The Gazette, Blackpool

9

WORLD'S END, WEST END,
WESTMORLAND

Dank and decrepit, Dartrey Road connected the World's End
to the Thames Embankment. Although the road was barely
an eighth of a mile long, hundreds of families were squeezed
into the houses divided into flats on each side of the street.
One side of the road consisted of a long continuous block
of terraced houses, four storeys high, comprising four flats
to each house, one to each floor. As the lower flats were
below pavement level, access was by the stone steps leading
down from the pavement. On the opposite side of the road
were three blocks of houses divided by two intersecting
streets. Every house was three storeys high and contained six
flats.

Each of these houses displayed the name of an English
county, which belied the run-down surroundings. I lived in the
end house, nearest the river, which bore the comically inappro-
priate name of Westmorland House – after what was England's remotest and most breathtakingly beautiful shire. I
remember once, as a small child, sitting on the kerbstone
beside another young lad. We both gazed up into the beautiful
sky, the sun having disappeared behind the Battersea factories
on the far side of the river. During sunsets like these, the
clouds looked like distant, rolling hills. Wistfully, the lad
exclaimed: 'Who's coming up in the mountains?' I recalled
this many years later while travelling through Cumbria (which
has now absorbed the ancient county of Westmorland) and
watching the sun setting against the mountains. Neither of us
knew that just around the corner from where we were sitting

had lived the artist J.M.W. Turner, the greatest painter of sunsets of all time. I am sure some of those Thames-side sunsets must have inspired him. (The American painter James Whistler had also been celebrated for his portrayals of old Chelsea, as well as for an evocative nocturne of Battersea Bridge.) Nor could I have known that later in my life I would be living in an area from which, on a clear day, the Lake District mountains are stunningly visible across Morecambe Bay.

We shared Westmorland House with five other families. As I was an only child, our family numbered just three, whereas most were at least double that size. Despite the crowded conditions, however, life for me as a school child was not unhappy. Exploiting the privilege of youth to the full, I would enter and leave most of the other flats in the house at will and was never discouraged from doing so. Indeed, it was an almost communal existence.

Life wasn't always easy, of course, and there were times when the thin partition walls of the flats were not conducive to family confidentiality or privacy. But this never seemed to cause embarrassment. Sometimes the weekly visit of the 'tallyman' to the next flat elicited no response to his continual knocking. On these occasions, he might emphasise his efforts by pleas of: 'Come on, Mrs May, I know you're in!' His persistence would eventually provoke an expletive in response, but this wouldn't cause Mrs May any problems in terms of her relations with her neighbours, nor, apparently, with the rejected tally-man. A couple of weeks later, having possibly received a few bob on account, he would be seen delivering another parcel to the flat. She would then emerge at the weekend resplendent in a new fur coat, albeit genuine rabbit! This was known as the 'glad and sorry' system – glad I've got it, sorry I can't pay!

There were other apt descriptions of the actions which some unfortunate families were forced into. One of these was known as the 'moonlight flit' or, more prosaically, the 'hurry-up'. The latter phrase needed no further explanation when you considered the haste necessary for a family to load all its possessions from a flat on to a barrow or cart, on a dark night

66

before the landlord realised that his back rent was gone for good.

In his classic novel, Robert Tressell has his main character, Frank Owen, describing his workmates in Mugsborough (Hastings) as philanthropists, benefactors in tattered trousers who willingly hand over the product of their labour to their employers – without recognising that socialism could level out these inequalities permanently. Despite Owen's attempts to educate them about the need for a change in the social structure, they believe the existing system is the natural order of the world and that the wealthy and powerful are entitled to exploit them. His famous description could just as easily have been applied to the people of the World's End, even if in a slightly different sense. Ragged-trousered they certainly were (except on Sundays), and some were truly philanthropists – though their philanthropy was reserved for those closest to them rather than for their employers.

Harry lived in the next-door flat to me and was a dozen years my senior. Every Saturday afternoon he would call for me to accompany him to a football match. Depending on which team was at home, this would alternate between Chelsea, half a mile away at Stamford Bridge, and Fulham, about a mile and a half to the west, at Craven Cottage by the river. He would pay my admission (sixpence) and always supplement this with a bag of sweets. When you consider what this meant to a small boy like me in the prevailing economic climate, and the fact that my benefactor had been an orphan from an early age – and so was himself a veteran in the survival stakes – he would certainly qualify as a fully paid-up member of any philanthropical society.

So, too, would John, a contemporary who lived in a top-floor flat above Harry. He took exception to the first cycle I ever owned. I had bought it for five shillings and parked it on the landing of the stairs which he had to use to reach his flat. He judged the machine, rightly, to be unsafe and in poor mechanical condition. The upshot was that he took me along to the local cycle agent in the King's Road and bought me a new Raleigh bike for cash (sixpence short of five pounds).

This was on the understanding that I repaid him a shilling a week from the wages from my paper-round. It took me a long time to repay, but it was a debt on which I never reneged.

While violence is often rife in a society in which hardship and poverty co-exist, it never played a dominant rôle in the life of the World's End. In all my many visits to the matches at Stamford Bridge and Craven Cottage, where the attendances at each were rarely below 30,000, I cannot recall any serious fights or disturbances, despite the fact that the fully-licensed bars were always open. If a fight between individuals did break out, it was invariably halted in a good-natured way by the onlookers. I did witness one such tussle between two antagonists which took place on the cinder track alongside the Stamford Bridge pitch before the kick-off, in full view of the thousands packed on to the terraces. The adversaries were unevenly matched physically, which soon became apparent to the smaller of the two. Acting on the premise that 'discretion is the better part of valour', he grabbed his larger opponent's testicles with both hands and hung on with all his might, to the hilarity and encouragement of the crowd and the obvious pain and helplessness of his opponent. Order (and relief for the bigger combatant) was restored by the swift arrival of the law, and by the subsequent ejection procession across the pitch to the exit; the good-humoured spectators considered the whole episode an *hors d'oeuvre* for the afternoon's more intentional entertainment.

At that time, a more formalised form of fighting – what has been described as 'the noble art of boxing' – was popular, and was also encouraged by the most unlikely institutions, such as the education authorities and even the Church of England. Perhaps they reasoned that it helped as a safety-valve to relieve the pent-up frustration and tension endemic in that society.

It was at the tender age of 12 that I became the five-and-a-half stone champion of the West London Schoolboys – a category my father appropriately and proudly described as 'whisker-weight'. I achieved this by winning three fights of three rounds' duration, each bout on the same night, at the

Duke of York's headquarters, which would later, of course, have Oswald Mosley's Blackshirts as its neighbours. It was an experience which, I can confirm, etched itself on my young mind for ever. Hardly less memorable were the pugilistic feats I undertook at the same time on behalf of the Church Lads' Brigade, of which I was a junior member (despite my somewhat unorthodox racial origins for a member of a muscularly Christian organisation). This troop was run under the auspices of St Mary Bolton's Church in the wealthy parish of Kensington, an elegant Anglican place of worship nestling in the green oasis between the two arms of The Boltons. Although separated geographically by just a few hundred yards from the World's End, in social terms it was on another planet and, as we saw in Chapter Five, its residences would be described by property dealers as 'very desirable'. But the genteel nature of the environment wasn't reflected in the personalities of those involved in the organisation of the Church Lads' Brigade, least of all in the boxing section.

This section was in the charge of an old former professional fighter known as 'Hoppy', who had received the nickname because one of his legs was shorter than the other – the result of his being knocked out of the Blackfriars Boxing Ring. This was a venue at which, in the past, old pros were reputed to have sought recognition by fighting for a purse as minimal as a bag of oranges! Hoppy certainly had his own ideas of how to toughen up his *protégés*. One of his favourite methods, which he called a 'battle royal', would take place at the end of every training session. It involved everyone present entering the ring, at which he would strike a bell as the signal for a free-for-all. The last survivor left in the ring would be considered the winner. But, although discretion played a significant part in early withdrawals from the fracas, it improved a lad's ability to evade – or, in less fortunate circumstances, absorb – punishment.

Hoppy didn't always adhere strictly to the Marquis of Queensbury Rules, as I painfully remember. Earning his living as a plumber, he was able to manufacture differently-shaped lead weights. When necessary, these were secreted about our person before the pre-contest weigh-in to avoid the possibility of disqualification on the grounds of being too light. As a result, we lighter lads were constantly giving weight away like top-weighted racehorses!

Despite our amateur status, Hoppy limped around many professional London halls, proudly exhibiting his team in tournaments, with a lot of success. This was because, as youngsters, we looked up to him and returned the devotion that, in his own way, he demonstrated towards us. We would visit many famous venues, such as Rugby Club, Notting Hill, Stadium Club, Holborn, and the Duke of York's, Sloane Square, as well as many of the public baths in the London boroughs. I am not qualified to assess any adverse effects, mentally or physically, that these experiences may or may not have had on my contemporaries. But I can, at least, confirm that I have never, since those early days, struck a fellow human being with a fist that was not encased in a boxing glove; nor have I experienced any apparent physical ill-effects.

Apart from the Established Church's support for the youthful boxing fraternity, religion didn't generally play a major part in the life of the World's End, most inhabitants only seeing the inside of a church at wedding and funeral services. There was, though, the lovable cleric known as 'Old Nuisance' who would roam the area shaking hands with everyone, particularly the children, bombarding them with jokes and riddles. The children loved him because he was a good man, and they were more discerning than their older peers, who mostly dismissed him as an eccentric. This was because, in their experience, they didn't equate goodness with churchmen, though there was an honourable tradition – particularly in the East End – of clergymen working in the community to foster the Judaeo-Christian principles of justice, equality before God and resistance to oppression.[1]

In the top flat above us in Westmorland House lived an apparently ageless taxi driver who was one of the original London cabbies, and his wife. He was known as 'Timmy Bang-Bang'. The ability of working-class people, particularly at such a harsh time, to describe each other so aptly through nicknames has always been a source of amusement and delight to me. If a person was short, for instance, he could become known as 'Little Legs'; if he was of smart appearance, the sobriquet might be 'Flash Harry'. I remember one member of the local corporation refuse staff who, on Sundays, would appear at the local, immaculately attired in a 50-shilling tailored suit, complete with watch-and-chain across the waistcoat and rings adorning his fingers. He was known, accurately, as the 'Golden Dustman'.

Timmy Bang-Bang's curious 'tab' was the result of a couple of factors. His surname was Timpson, and the suffix was due to an unfortunate episode involving the law. At one time, he had decided, for economic reasons, to ferment his own wine. Perhaps the gentry whom he whisked around the West End in his cab had not been tipping as well as usual, or possibly they were more patient in waiting for their change. (Taxis in those days had no heaters or side-windows at the front to protect the driver, so cabbies would wear many waistcoats, with their money in the pockets of the innermost layer – which could cause a long delay in transactions on a cold night.) He had seemingly bottled some of his demon brew prematurely, and the liquid had expanded rapidly, resulting in a cork smashing through the window of his flat in the middle of the night, rousing the whole neighbourhood. This was quickly inflated on the grapevine into reports that a shot had been fired. When the police arrived, the only information the greatly-shaken Timmy could produce during the interview was: 'All I know was that there was a bloody big bang-bang!'

Whatever the World's Enders lacked in religious fervour, they compensated for in their expressions of patriotism and support of anything associated with royalty. During royal jubilees, coronations or marriages, large banners would stretch high above the streets between the little houses, emblazoned with such slogans as 'Poor but Loyal'. There was no disputing the accuracy of the first epithet, but the second described only a section of the population, albeit possibly a majority. There were some sceptics who could be heard to say, during the political debates held regularly at the World's End speakers' corner, that it was 'being so loyal that kept them so bloody poor'!

Patriotism in Dartrey Road was personified for me by Fred, who, despite being a member of a large family crowded into a small flat, would always appear on Sunday morning resplendent in full regimental dress. As an enthusiastic member of the Territorials, he wore a brilliant red sash over his blue tunic, with glittering golden buttons and buckled leather belt. Coupled with the thick red stripe down the razor-creased trousers that rested on his black, shining boots – with a small red-banded peaked cap to crown the uniform – it completed what seemed to me a truly military *ensemble*. As youngsters, with some admiration and much envy, we would watch him march down the street towards the Embankment on his way to the Battersea Drill Hall. I suppose we identified him with the words of a song they taught us at Ashburnham School, which began:

> I am a Briton bold and free,
> I love my country well;
> And proud am I, as all should be,
> In such a land to dwell.

Unfortunately, a few years later at the start of the Second World War, Fred's uniform had to be replaced with a mundane khaki, and he was posted to other parts. But he re-appeared in a few weeks in 'mufti'; he had apparently been invalided out of the Army because of bad feet!

Ironically, many of my young contemporaries who had been exposed to – but avoided – the allure of military life were later to experience one of the cruellest fates to befall a British soldier, and one of the nation's most humiliating military defeats. At the outbreak of war, most of them were enlisted into the Middlesex Regiment and were embarked for the Far East. After the Japanese invasion of Malaya in December 1941, they were delivered into the hands of the invaders almost immediately – at the surrender of Singapore to a 25,000-strong enemy force on 15 February 1942 – scarcely firing a shot. The few who survived the appalling conditions in the prisoner-of-war camps, and returned later to their homes (those homes that were still intact after the years of bombing), were quietly re-absorbed into their families' lives. There, at least, the broken minds and bodies received the care and succour that can only be truly provided by those who have themselves survived a history of deprivation.[2]

If, as children, we enjoyed singing that patriotic song, it was due less to love of country (though we did love it, in our own way) than to the fact that it was rendered every Empire Day – which meant a half-day holiday from school. My own first contact with the British Empire during the war years caused me to re-evaluate my whole understanding of imperialism and the concept of patriotism that had been presented to us during our formative years. But that is another story . . .

NOTES

1 One of the best-known was the Reverend John Groser, an Anglo-Catholic priest who worked for 40 years in the heart of the community in the East End. A prophetic Christian socialist, he played a central rôle in the resistance to fascism in the 1930s, and was vicar of Christ Church, Watney Street, when the Battle of Cable Street took place. In the 1930s he saw fascism as 'the greatest menace to the Christian religion in the world today'. During the Blitz he and other High Anglican clergy played a pivotal part in ministering to the social and spiritual needs of their parishioners in the slums, helping cement the bonds of community that withstood the nightly bombardment by German bombers. Unconcerned about promotion, Groser was not afraid to break the rules and did not shrink from conflict with authority. He died in 1966, remembered as much for his pioneering pastoral and social work as for his theological thought.

2 By a remarkable coincidence, another of the units captured on the fall of Singapore was the 137th (Army) Field Regiment of the Royal Artillery – the 'Blackpool Regiment'. It was composed almost exclusively of recruits from the Fylde Coast area, which was later to become my adopted home, and its PoWs suffered grievously at the

hands of their brutal captors, some of the Blackpool men being used as slave labour on the infamous Burma-Siam railway. The resort remains a stronghold of the Far Eastern Prisoners' of War Association and the Burma Star.

10

'OLE BILL'

'Ole Bill' was not, as might be presumed from today's London-located TV cop shows, the local bobby; he was, in fact, the community's 'coalie'. He lived in the shadow of the power station in a small terraced house opposite the school, a stone's throw from the local pub, the Balloon Tavern. It was so named as it stood on the site of what had once been the launching pad for a balloon.

The whole area had originally been the site of the Cremorne Gardens, established on the banks of the Thames by Viscount Cremorne. These had been the festival gardens in the times of Nell Gwynne and her lover 'Charlie' – King Charles II. The industrial landscape was now the complete antithesis to the arcadia that must once have existed there, but the original wrought-iron gates of the gardens were still in place – though they now, rather ignominiously, adorned the entrance to the Watney's brewery a few hundred yards away, just off the King's Road.

Looking back over all those years, I would have to conclude that Ole Bill was perhaps the toughest and hardest man I could remember. Yet he was also, possibly, one of the most content, notwithstanding the adversities of that era – and despite what could have been considered to be the burden of a large family to support. Although the grim townscape exhibited few echoes of the former festivities, there were times when Ole Bill came close to emulating the atmosphere of those seventeenth-century royal junketings – albeit on a budget that was microscopical by comparison.

His day started every morning, except Sunday, at 5 a.m. in the Balloon Tavern. The early opening was permitted as the coal wharf was on the docks opposite the pub and, due to the vagaries of the Thames tides, special licensing laws allowed the dockers to take their refreshment in the small hours. Ole Bill's itinerary was one of metronomic regularity. After his early refreshment, he would cross the road to the wharf stables and harness his shire horse to its cart. Next he visited the coal tip where he would load the cart with sacks weighing between a half- and two-hundredweight, always to the maximum capacity. Then he would begin trundling around the streets of Chelsea, distributing his load. I never ceased to be amazed at his prowess at being able to lump two-hundredweight sacks of coal, which seemed as big as he was, up perhaps four flights of narrow stairs, with hardly any space to manoeuvre, especially when he reached the flats themselves. Depending on the season, his round could be repeated twice or even more in one day.

But every evening, come what may, he could be found ensconced once more in the 'snug' back at his beloved Balloon with his friends and workmates. They would smoke shag tobacco in clay pipes, costing a penny each, the stems of which they would break off about an inch from the bowls, presumably to allow their nostrils greater access to the acrid smoke. Amid the haze that resulted, they would mull over the day's events, play dominoes and drink their ale at fourpence a pint. Modern medics and other health specialists would now cite this type of lifestyle as being the perfect passport to an early grave: Ole Bill was 96 when he died!

There was one day in the year, however, which even Ole Bill and his case-hardened comrades looked forward to with particular relish – the annual 'Beano'. Every pay-day during the year, workers would make payments to the landlord – known as the 'Governor' – towards the cost of the great day out. The destination and means of conveyance never varied: Southend-on-Sea by 'charabanc'.

Before one especially memorable day out, Ole Bill and his companions, as was their custom, arrived for the early opening of the Balloon to ensure they were in the right spirit for the journey when the charabanc turned up a couple of hours later, at 8 a.m. (It should be pointed out that the revellers were all male; the phrase 'chauvinist pig' was yet to be coined. The older women of the time never seemed to venture abroad, and there were mothers of large families who – despite living within 50 miles of the coast all their lives – had never even seen the sea.) When the charabanc arrived, Ole Bill had rather overdone his 'mood-preparedness' and was, in the vernacular, 'legless'. Not only had his mates to carry the many wooden crates of beer aboard; they also had to manhandle him and a couple of his equally inebriate friends.

The Beano ritual was always identical. The first stop was invariably just outside London to allow the revellers to relieve themselves and also to top up from the on-board beer, as the pubs would not yet be open. Ole Bill, who was probably showing signs of recovery by now, was 'topped-up' and reduced again to his former state. The next stop was always the Halfway House Tavern, which was, unsurprisingly, halfway to Southend. As the licensing hours had now begun, everyone left the coach and invaded the bars, including the well-lubricated coalie, who again had to be carried. Usually they reached their final destination in the centre of Southend before the pubs closed for the afternoon, but this was not imperative as the revellers generally still had enormous quantities of refreshments on board. After getting off the vehicle, they would always manage a 'knees-up' before pouring on to 'the Front'. I will never forget the time when a very tall, thin man, with a bowler hat pulled down over his ears, danced and girated as he sang his version of the old Yiddish song 'Abie, my boy'! The last word of the title was pronounced, with typical Yiddisher gusto, as 'phboy . . .'

Just as my adopted home of Blackpool is the great working-class tourist capital of the North, so Southend, on the Essex coast where the Thames broadens out to meet the sea, has long been the southern proletariat's playground. Two hundred years ago it didn't even exist. It was oysters that brought Southend into being, along with the trend for fashionable visitors to decamp to the health-giving ozone and salt water of the seaside in the late eighteenth century. For the World's

77

Enders, the customary invasion of the cockle, whelk and oyster bars was the only chance in the year they had to emulate, by swallowing the crustacean delicacies, the lifestyle of Charles II in the Cremorne Gardens almost 300 years earlier.

A century before our charabanc excursion, Southend was only a short journey by boat from London – though, in those days, passengers had to be carried ashore by burly fishermen. The arrival of the railway in March 1856 opened up the resort to working-class visitors, and so the tribal loyalties of central London were soon translated to the coast. Southend was – and remains – a curious mixture of the stylish and crude, the elegance of its Regency terraces contrasting with the bank holiday bustle of Marine Parade.

After sampling the seafood, we would pour on to Southend Pier, which modestly described itself as 'the longest in the world'. A mile and a quarter long, the structure suffered severe damage to the pierhead buildings in a fire in 1976. Another favourite port of call was the Kursaal, with its multiplicity of amusements. An Edwardian vision of a dance hall, at the eastern end of the promenade, the Kursaal was characterised by its magnificently ornate colonial-style pillared central dome. Then, in the early evening, we would all return to the car park and the waiting 'chara'. There were times when this waiting had been in vain and the return journey had to be undertaken with fewer passengers than had been on the outward trip. This time, though, everyone was accounted for – after some delay, naturally – although one or two travellers, including Ole Bill, owed their presence on the bus to the strong arms and backs of their coalie colleagues.

On the journey home, the highlight was always the return visit to the Halfway House where, with dozens of other charabanc-borne travellers, the singing and dancing continued until the inevitable call of 'time, gentlemen, please'. As can be imagined, this imprecation had to be repeated many times: the expertise needed by the publican and his staff to cajole recalcitrant customers outside and finally get the doors closed would have been an object lesson to anyone considering a career as a mediator or Foreign Office diplomat.

When they reached the World's End – and journey's end –
it was agreed that, because of the uncertain state of Ole Bill's
equilibrium, the charabanc would stop first at his house to
allow him to be carried straight off and up the stairs to his
bedroom. This was duly accomplished, and the journey was
then completed, round the corner to the Balloon, where many
welcoming wives and friends were gathered.

The main point of this narrative is simple. Having saved his
money all year for this special day, but spending most of it
being carried around by his friends, Ole Bill could never
afterwards recall having been on the Beano! But there is a
second, more serious, message. Anyone who would hasten to
pass judgement on Ole Bill and his colleagues should think
twice before doing so. Born into grinding poverty, he had
survived the hell of Flanders and, with a loving wife, managed
to bring up, in terrible conditions, a large family who adored
him and some of whom he outlived. He died a few years after
his wife, having been cared for to the end by devoted daugh-
ters. These were the type of people whom many years later,
during the 1984/5 miners' strike, Lord Stockton – the former
Tory Prime Minister Harold Macmillan – would describe as
'the salt of the earth'.

It would be wrong not to record an episode involving one
of Ole Bill's contemporaries which further typified the life and
times of the day. It was sometimes possible, though not usual,
for a single person (always a man) to be able to afford a full
week's holiday in Southend. This could be the result of some
unexpected financial windfall, such as the residue from an
insurance policy after the death of a relative or an unusually
successful bet on a horse. It was never possible by accumulat-
ing savings from the weekly wage packet. (The paradox now
is that, as wage packets have expanded, the number of visitors
staying for a full week in Southend – as in Blackpool – has
declined in the face of competition from overseas resorts.)

On one of the Balloon's Beanos, it proved more than usually
difficult to round up the revellers for the evening departure
from Southend. More than one body was carried on to the
parked charabanc. Indeed, when they got back to the Balloon,

some were still not fully recovered. This didn't present any great problems, however, as there were many willing hands among the reception committee to help guide the over-indulgent to their front doors. One of those the worse for wear, who didn't seem to have anyone to collect him, was quickly recognised and promptly received the help of a couple of volunteers to escort him to his bed. When they delivered him to his doorstep, they had some difficulty arousing the household. Eventually the front door was opened by a woman in her nightdress who, after taking one look at the swaying figure before her, exclaimed: 'What's he doing here? He only went to Southend this morning – for a week!'

11

'GARY'

Innate humour has always been a potent ingredient of the British working-class character, particularly in the inner cities, where living in such proximity seems to accentuate the characteristic. I have found this to be true whether it is applied to Cockneys, Scousers, Geordies, Brummies or any other city-dwellers. That quality was certainly to the fore in the Chelsea slums of the 1920s and 1930s.

Humour was an essential tool for survival in those conditions. People had to be able to laugh in adversity, and they did this mostly at themselves or each other. They would find amusement, for instance, in the eternal struggle between the street bookmakers, who provided them with a usually forlorn hope of financial relief, and the plain-clothes police.

Urchin humour was also responsible for giving 'Gary' his adopted name; his real one, improbably, was Leonard but, during a history lesson at school, the name of the Italian patriot Garibaldi was mentioned in the class. This prompted a young wit to turn to Leonard – who always had his hair cropped short, except for a tuft up front, in a style known as the 'fourpenny all-off' – and pronounce him 'Gary-Baldhead'. He was known by this name until a small schoolmate calling for him one morning asked his mother: 'Is Gary-Baldhead coming out?' He received the irate reply: 'His name ain't bloody Gary-Baldhead and he ain't bloody well coming out!' At this, the door was slammed shut with such ferocity that he was known for ever after as simply 'Gary'.

He was the youngest of four brothers and a sister in a stalwart socialist household. While the whole family could have been described as unorthodox or even eccentric, they were at least independent, in the true sense of the word. And their deeply-ingrained loathing of those who controlled the system in which they were forced to exist was not conducive to their keeping 'a noiseless tenor of their way', to quote from *Elegy* again.

In his later teens, Gary was at times given to seeking only his own company in order, as he put it, 'to wine with Bacchus'. When he was in one these moods, he would take himself off in the evening to one of the quiet little pubs in the more prosperous back-streets of Chelsea where you could sometimes, in those days, spend an evening in the company of the artists and *bona fide* Bohemians who frequented the area.

On the way along the Embankent from his home, he would pass through Cheyne Walk, with its imposing mansion-like houses and balconies that overlooked expansive front gardens protected by ornate wrought-iron gates. Inside lived senior members of the judiciary, government and other prominent society figures.[1] Not that we normally caught sight of members of this exclusive fraternity, although there was one exception. This was an old dowager who would appear periodically on a front balcony, much the worse for drink, and who would sway dangerously while screeching at anyone who happened to be passing: 'Get back to your hovels!' While I have no idea if Lloyd George, who was himself the son of a provincial schoolmaster, ever heard her exhortations – or, if he did, what his reactions were – I can verify at least that she wasn't Gary's favourite old lady.

On one evening when Gary, having indulged himself generously, was weaving his lonely way home along moonlit Cheyne Walk, he decided that a certain piece of cherubic stonemasonry in a cloistered front garden would be an ideal retreat at which to carry out nature's imperative call. In fact, his proximity to the cherub evidently heightened his appreciation of its artistry so much that he decided to take it home. This he succeeded in doing, although it surpasses my understanding – and probably did his also – how he managed to carry on his back a statue weighing well over a hundredweight a distance of more than a mile, unobserved by the law, and deposit it in his own backyard.

Like Billy and Ron's father in Chapter Eight, his dad was an old soldier who would recount endlessly (as long as the ale was kept flowing) his memories of the many campaigns in which he had served. He was accustomed to the curious occurrences in and around his family. But even he was somewhat shaken, as he looked out of the window of the back scullery next morning before washing and shaving, to see a chubby stone cherub staring back at him. It wasn't so much the presence of the *objet d'art* that perplexed him but rather that, despite endless questioning, Gary maintained a complete ignorance of how the figure had got there. After a few weeks, the statue became an accepted part of its surroundings, and the mystery over its presence was apparently forgotten. It seemed, indeed, that the old man had grown quite attached to it, and almost proud; it was, whatever else, a unique possession in that part of the city.

His pride of ownership, though, was rudely destroyed a few weeks later when, as he was about to begin his morning ablutions, he looked through the scullery window and saw a patch of bare ground where the sculpture had stood. He never saw it again and, despite all his efforts to extract information from his son, its disappearance – like its arrival – always remained a mystery.

What actually happened was that Gary had been struck by an attack of remorse at his actions. Returning home late one evening from one of his lone carousings, he had gazed at the cherubic countenance in the moonlight and decided to make amends for its removal. He had retraced his journey of a few weeks before, and succeeded in returning it, again unobserved, to its previous position in the garden in Cheyne Walk.

Many times over the years I have tried to picture Gary's staggering strolls along the Embankment and to imagine the thoughts of anyone fortunate enough to have passed him. But, most of all, I have tried to visualise the reactions of the sculpture's owners on waking up one morning to see its return and to discover that it had only been (as Gary explained to me) 'borrowed for a while'.

My last encounter with Gary took place years later, after

83

the war. On a sentimental journey through Chelsea one Sunday morning, I met him on the Embankment between Albert and Battersea Bridges where, with other artists, he was exhibiting his work. By this time, he had taken to poetry and painting, and was hoping the sales of his pictures would help him eke out a livelihood. I asked him how successful he had been, and he told me he did manage to sell some paintings but was having little luck with his poems. With characteristic humour, he added: 'I think, perhaps, I should paint poems . . .'

NOTE

1   No. 96 Cheyne Walk was the home of Bryan and Diana Guinness: it was at a party there to celebrate her 22nd birthday in 1932 that Oswald Mosley was reputed to have made a proposal to his future wife that their relationship be put on a more formal footing. I recall that at one time the former coalition Prime Minister, the famous Liberal David Lloyd George, was also one of these fortunate Cheyne Walk *habitués*.

12

SIX MEN IN A CAR

On the morning of my 17th birthday, my most pressing task was to visit the local Post Office, pay 7s/6d and obtain my first driving licence. So, despite not having driven any vehicle on any public road, I was now able to do so whenever I wished, in those pre-driving test days. This raised my reputation with my street-mates, who insisted that six of us club together and hire a car for the weekend. They ignored any reluctance on my part; while I had shunted cars around the garage workshop, I had not actually driven one on the road. It was enough that I had a licence and, after all, they said, 'aren't you a mechanic?'

So, one Friday evening, I met Joe (who was the oldest of us, having reached the grand age of 20) and we paid a visit to a small garage in the Dawes Road, Fulham, to arrange the hire of a car for the following Sunday. The deal was struck with consummate ease, the proprietor interested only in glancing at my licence, while he received the one pound note from Joe for the day's hire. The cost would eventually be split six ways among us, though not necessarily in equal amounts, as our friendship was such that money was unimportant. Those who could afford paid, and those who couldn't were included anyway! There would, of course, also be the expense of the petrol but, as ROP (Russian Oil Produce) was only tenpence a gallon, this was not a formidable obstacle.

The car to be hired was out at the time of our transaction – much to my relief – and the proprietor explained that it was an Austin Tourer, which would be parked in a lock-up next to the workshop for collection on the Sunday morning. After giving us the lock-up key, he told us to be quiet when we collected it as he lived above the premises and didn't want to be disturbed on his only day off.

At the crack of dawn on the Sunday, Joe and I arrived at the premises and quietly opened the garage doors. I was filled with trepidation at my first sight of the car; completely filling the lock-up, it appeared huge and awesome. It had two large chromium headlamps that glared at me from an enormous radiator to which they were connected by thick metal supports. Underneath, a formidably heavy-looking starting handle protruded, in front of which was mounted a front bumper that looked capable of dealing with an irresistible force. The car had two windscreens, one of which was behind the driver for the convenience of the back-seat passengers; it could be folded away when not needed. Likewise, the canvas hood could also be folded back and the side cellophane windows removed during fine weather. Both side running-boards had a spare wheel fitted, and on one side was a heavy-duty 12-volt battery.

Climbing over the bonnet and front wing to sit in the driving seat, I looked at the control levers mounted on top of the steering-wheel with apprehension. These consisted of a throttle, advance and retard ignition control, and mixture-control levers, which led me to expect some initial starting problems. After releasing the heavy transmission handbrake, Joe and I managed to pull the machine out of the lock-up by yanking on the front bumper. Because of a slight gradient, we were able to push it a hundred yards along the road out of the hearing of the garage's sleeping proprietor. Repeated cranking with the large starting handle – combined with various permutations of the positions of levers – had failed to start the infernal engine, but I then made an important discovery. Accidentally treading on the edge of the thick coconut matting on the driver's floor, I discovered a self-starter button. With further jiggling of the levers, combined with flooding of the carburettor, this eventually resulted in the engine starting, and we headed towards Lots Road power station, where we were to meet the others.

While Joe seemed to be in his element, and almost jubilant at the way things were shaping up, I was worried about my failure to change gears noiselessly. The gearbox was known as a 'crash-type' and gear-changing was carried out via a 'gate-change' on the top of the gearbox and the bottom of the gear-lever. As there was no synchro-mesh mechanism in the box, a system known as 'double-declutching' had to be used to ensure a quiet gear change, by synchronising the speed of the gears. Changing gear downwards needed the most skill, and attempting to do this while descending a steep hill was later to lead to a hair-raising incident during our day out.

As it was early Sunday morning, the roads were initially empty and, apart from the occasional crashing of gears, the couple of miles to the Lots Road were negotiated successfully. However, the Balloon Tavern, which was our rendezvous, stood next to a bend in that road. As I negotiated this at speed, I was suddenly confronted by an enthusiastic four-strong reception committee greeting our arrival in the middle of the road. Brake mechanisms on cars at that time were unsophisticated, comprising a cam in the brake drum which, when turned by the brake rod via the pedal, just pressed the brake shoes against the drum without any hydraulic or 'self-energising' assistance. So brake efficiency left a lot to be desired on most cars.

Sammy, Dickie, Peter and Sid, unaware of the technical shortcomings of the vehicle's braking system, escaped injury by leaping out of the way in different directions. It was only the first calamity during what was to be an extremely eventful day. They piled enthusiastically into the car with no recriminations against their driver: their confidence in me was complete. I wished I could have shared it!

Although the engine was warm by now, constant use of the self-starter, combined once more with permutations of the levers, again failed to start it. Eventually I discovered that if Joe opened the bonnet and sat on the wing – while he flooded the carburettor by lifting the float chamber needle, at the same time as I waggled the throttle from the driver's seat – we were able to restart the confounded thing. This procedure, which was to be repeated throughout the day whenever we came to a halt – unless I succeeded in keeping the engine 'revving' –

proved to be just one of my major problems. Traffic lights at that period were non-existent, and every main junction was controlled by a policeman on point duty. Geographically, this was to have an effect on our journey across London because I strayed from our intended route to avoid main junctions.

We had intended to head for the Sussex coast but, having missed out a couple of bridges across the Thames, we eventually crossed the Westminster Bridge heading for Kent! By this time, I had decided to point the car towards the coast and head anywhere, so long as we arrived at the sea. I was beginning to grow more confident as the passengers became more boisterous. As we passed a dozen or more beefy young men from a cycling club, many ribald remarks were exchanged. My co-travellers obviously felt that, owing to our greater speed, they had no need to be inhibited in the exchanges. Unfortunately, however, a few miles further along we had decided to pull into a roadside café for refreshments. As we were leaving, while we were absorbed in the complex restarting procedure, the cycling club appeared in the distance. Most of our party discreetly melted away, leaving just Joe and me bent beneath the bonnet over the recalcitrant engine. Much to our relief, the burly bicyclists, with their heads down and toes well dug into their pedals, sped past without noticing us.

Around midday, though, we realised we were completely lost. With no definite destination in view, just happy to be speeding through Kentish countryside, we encountered our next near-calamity. After managing to climb a steep hill in bottom gear, we turned a right-hand bend and were immediately confronted by a sign that read: 'Warning – steep hill – engage a low gear'. Immediately I tried to carry out the procedure known as 'double-declutching'. This meant pressing the clutch pedal down, moving the gear lever into neutral, revving the engine with the pedal released in an effort to synchronise the engine speed with the lower gears in the box, depressing the clutch pedal to engage the low gear and releasing the pedal again when successful. This would allow the engine to act as a brake when going down the hill. Unfortunately, I had not yet acquired the skill to do this. Having put the gear into neutral, I could not then, despite continually crashing the gears, engage either a lower gear or even get back into top gear. With now no braking effect of the engine on the road wheels, the heavily-laden car continued unencumbered down the hill at an ever-increasing speed. Application of the never-very-efficient footbrake, and the even-less-effective transmission handbrake, had little effect on our downhill dash, except to produce an ever-stronger smell of burning asbestos linings as the brake drums grew hotter. It was the encounter with an acute right-hand bend that finally reduced me to complete panic as I realised that no earthly force would allow us and the car to continue along the route of that road. As the road changed direction, we continued at full speed ahead, fortunately up a banking, over shrubs and bushes – finally coming to a halt perched at a precarious angle against a small tree trunk.

While the experience, putting it mildly, subdued my ego, it didn't have a similar effect on the passengers, who treated it with great hilarity; nor did it even diminish their confidence in their driver's abilty. Their feelings, however, were not shared by a very shaken old farmhand who arrived on the scene complete with a shepherd's crook, entreating me to: 'Never ever come down that hill again at that bloody speed, son!'

After a lot of pushing and rocking, we were able to get the car back on the road and, as it was built like a small military tank, there appeared to be no obvious damage. While we waited for the brake drums and mechanism to cool down, we discussed our eventual destination. By this time, the lads had considered that we were taking too long to reach the coast in the direction in which we were travelling. We decided to head back to the Thames and make, inevitably, for the Cockney Mecca of Southend-on-Sea across the river. Although we managed to reach the crossing at the Woolwich ferry without further mishap, we were to encounter more difficulties during the boarding and disembarkation procedures. As we were at the head of the queue, we were the first to be summoned aboard. Unfortunately the engine stalled halfway across the boarding platform and the combined efforts of all concerned, including the ferry crew, failed to restart it. Once again, much pushing and shoving was needed to move the stubborn vehicle aross the deck into position.

When we reached the north side of the river, the engine was still as obstinate. As we were to be the first to leave the ferry, the entire crew – including, by this time, the captain – had to manoeuvre the car off the boat to allow the other travellers to drive off. The passengers' frustration was intense, but it failed to match that of the crew, who were uninhibited in voicing their feelings towards us and the car in time-worn nautical language.

Eventually, we managed to restart the vehicle and ventured forth towards our latest destination of Southend. On the way, however, we decided again to change direction and follow the signposts to Canvey Island, another favourite day-out destination for Londoners, which was nearer. We arrived there after only a minor mishap – slightly scraping the offside rear corner panel of a corporation bus. This didn't cause us any problems, however, as we took a quick decision not to stop to investigate.

By now, we were getting hungry and thirsty so I parked at a tavern alongside a large fun fair. The pub had a roomy lounge, in the centre of which stood an obviously well-maintained piano. Predictably, the instrument proved an attraction for our party after a couple of drinks and Dickie, who was an accomplished amateur pianist, needed little persuasion when he was urged to 'get on the ivories'. It wasn't long before the customers in the lounge were transformed from a somewhat sedate assembly into a jovial crowd enjoying a party atmosphere. This wasn't surprising because my friends, notwithstanding their lack of possessions and their humble backgrounds, were eager entertainers with melodious voices. But, above all, they had the attribute described in the words of a popular song that was not to be written for another three decades: 'They were young and bound to have their way.'

Such was our popularity with our fellow patrons and the management that both showed their appreciation by ensuring the refreshment flowed plentifully. This was just as well because, true to form, our combined funds were limited. After what must have been a couple of hours' revelry, the capriciousness of youth – accentuated by the lure of the nearby fairground – asserted itself. Amid the fond farewells from our newly-made friends, we descended, well fortified, on the amusements.

It was amid the cacophony of the swings and merry-go-rounds that we met a young gypsy fortune-teller, whom I shall never forget. This wasn't because she was such a lovely young girl, though she was; not even because she obviously took a shine to us, and read all our palms free of charge; it was because of the uncanny accuracy of her predictions. She told us that we were all going to travel far in the future – but in different directions – and until then we would be happy. Her prophecies could not have been more prescient. Within a few years, we were to be overtaken by the great catastrophe of world war, over which we had no control, and put in different services scattered across the globe. Four of the six of us were never to return.

It was early evening when, tired but content and wearing American sailor-hats, we bade farewell to the fair and made our way back to the car. Although the headlamps were large and looked impressive, I had no experience of their efficiency in the dark. Indeed, I had no real experience of driving any car with its headlamps on. So I thought it best to get nearer home before acquiring that expertise. With Joe's help, I again restarted the engine and pointed the vehicle towards London.

For a while, our homeward journey went smoothly; the passengers, no doubt feeling the effects of their unusual day, were relaxing in a manner befitting experienced car travellers. But this mood didn't last as we started to leave the countryside. They began to take notice of the more urban surroundings and urged me to to 'see what it can do'; so, against my better judgement, I put my foot down. I couldn't have picked a worse time to try to break any land-speed records because we flashed across what turned out to be a main road, on the pavement of which stood two extremely large policemen. Even worse, we had sped into a *cul-de-sac*.

91

Having, with great difficulty, turned the car round, we re-approached the main road, but our access was now blocked by the two officers standing in the middle of the road. Silently, they stood at each side of the front doors while they read the writing on the bands of our American sailor-style headware. After what seemed an eternity, one shouted to the other in an incredulous tone: 'Peel him a grape!' Whereupon the other PC, standing by my driver's door, repeated aloud the inscription on my hat – 'I'm no angel' – adding with venomous emphasis: 'You bloody well soon will be, son, if you come across that road again at that speed!' They received my answers to their further questions with an air of quizzical tolerance – probably the result of the sight of my week-old licence. This tolerance was widespread in the constabulary at that time, and a law-breaking youth was more likely to receive a clip round the ear than a summons. Consequently, we all received a dressing-down to end all dressings-down by both bobbies before we were allowed to proceed. The resumption of our journey was somewhat marred by one of the portly PCs, who had been helping restart the car, having to jump hastily out of the way as the machine lurched unexpectedly forward. But we were on our way and didn't dare look back to see the consequences.

As we entered the London suburbs, twilight was beginning to give way to darkness and our journey was now becoming relatively incident-free. This was partly due to my increased confidence in handling the gearbox and also because point-duty policemen were generally not on duty after dark. I was, therefore, able to take a direct route, without diversions, towards Chelsea and the World's End. As we crossed the Thames over the Vauxhall Bridge and turned along the Embankment towards the tall Lots Road power station chimneys, for the first time I began to feel the effects of the pressures of an eventful day that would live in my memory.

After we had dropped the lads off at the Balloon Tavern, Joe accompanied me to return the vehicle to the garage in the Dawes Road. I did manage to rehouse the monster in its tight-fitting lock-up, with only a slight contact between the indestructible bumper and a door pillar, but as no-one was present we quietly closed the garage doors and left. That night I slept the sleep of the exhausted.

We had many more enjoyable outings, though not in that same car, and, I can confirm, no harm was done to property or person during these excursions. I like to feel that any pleasure my friends derived from our trips was deserved. For most of them, it was to be one of their last opportunities to experience a little happiness before they were to pay with their lives the terrible price that war always demands of the flower of youth.

13

CRIES FROM THE STREET AND THE HEART

The cacophonous chorus of sounds that reverberated through the hustle and bustle of pre-war Chelsea could be divided into two distinct categories: the noise of the traders and hawkers, and the more mellifluous tones of the street entertainers and buskers. All were true professionals; if they failed to collect in the 'ha'pennies and pennies', they would starve. They, and the sounds they made – whether raucous or melodic – were an organic part of the communal life of the area, and without them life would have been a much more miserable affair.

For me, one of the most pleasant memories was of the gypsy families who, during the summer, would patrol the streets laden with armfuls of lavender, the whole family singing in turn as they walked along, in a sort of pre-TV advertising jingle:

> Will you buy my sweet blooming lavender?
> It's 16 blue branches for one penny.
> You buy it once, you'll buy it twice;
> It makes your pocket handkerchiefs smell very nice.
> It's 16 blue branches for one penny.

Then there was the 'Muffin Man' who, every Sunday, would walk the streets balancing a large wooden tray on his head and carrying a bell which he shook vigorously between his cries of 'Muffins!'. Always a delight to me, too, was the 'Cats-meat Man'. He would carry a colossal cane basket in front of him, supported by a thick leather strap around his neck. Fitted

94

on the basket was a metal hook which allowed him to mount it periodically on the front railings of the houses as he advertised and dispensed his wares. He would cut the horse-meat into small pieces during these stops and push them on to sharpened wooden sticks, for which he charged tuppence apiece. But my most comic recollection of him was the miaowing of the army of cats that would follow him as he made his rounds. It speaks volumes for the local people that, despite the difficulties they had in feeding their families, they still insisted on supplying sustenance for their pets – thus enabling the 'Cats-meat Man' to earn a living.

There was another horse-meat vendor in a shop in the sinisterly-named World's End Passage. Formerly known as 'The Way Between the Poles', it had once contained a handful of cottages and a foundry that made siege guns and recast the bells of Chelsea Old Church. The passage was a narrow lane that started between the World's End pub and the Prince of Wales Cinema – the 'Bug 'Ole' of fond memory – and ran down to the river. Outside, the shop looked like a cavern and, inside, it resembled a dimly-lit Dickensian Fagin's den – with an odour to match. From its low ceiling, hanging by hooks, were slung hunks of horse-meat ready to be sliced for sale. Stacked beneath, on the stone floor, were sacks of old rags and a miscellany of jam-jars and junk which, at times, reached such proportions that it was difficult to get in. This was because the shop doubled as a receiving base for the produce collected daily by the local rag-and-bone men, known as 'totters'. These traders, either pushing hand-barrows or seated on their horse-drawn or donkey-drawn carts, contributed a counterpoint to the daily chorus of cries of Chelsea, as they tried to eke out an existence around its streets.

Some of the traders' cries would have meant nothing to the uninitiated ear, such as the bellowing voice that proclaimed: 'Eeh-eye-abbeys!' This, translated into strict BBC English, would be: 'Here are your wild rabbits!' The hawker would push a heavy two-wheeled barrow, on which were carried dozens of rabbits, hung by their rear legs from broomsticks. After you had made your choice, he would skin it on the spot, and I cannot remember the cost of the largest rabbit being more than a bob.

As well as these, there were battalions of other vendors patrolling the pavements and streets with every kind of fruit and vegetable imaginable. In the summer these were brought in from the Kent countryside by all manner of conveyance, ranging from horse-drawn carts to lorries. Each trader would sing out his wares in his own, individual style. They were certainly not inhibited by anything akin to the modern Trades Descriptions Act. The man who sold the winkles and shrimps on a Sunday, for instance, would advertise them with an additional cry of: 'Right off the boat!' Which, considering the distance from Chelsea to any part of the coast, could not have been strictly true. At intervals, he would add that he didn't 'store them under the bed' – which must have been a reference to the storage practices of a rival trader. Near the Riley Arms was the 'Hole in the Wall' – a literal description – where eels and mashed potatoes were sold. Occasionally, live eels would escape and slither aross the King's Road, slowing the traffic (which wasn't particularly fast at that time in any case).

As a small boy, I was particularly thrilled by the arrival of the 'Okey-Pokey Man'. He sold a cheap form of ice-cream which he dispensed from large barrels mounted on the rear of a horse-drawn cart. Between long spells of serving (his wares were very popular with the youngsters), he would cry:

> Okey-Pokey, penny a lump,
> It's the stuff to make you jump.

Saturday evening was the peak trading period in the shops around the World's End. Most fresh food shops had open fronts, and trading would continue until after 10 p.m. Particularly late openers were the butchers, who, as refrigeration was not then widely available, would have to auction off all their unsold meat at the end of the day's trading. There was much banter at these auctions, especially as some of the lady shoppers would have earlier 'dallied and dillied' in the World's End pub for a measure of spirits known as a 'half-quarten'.

And some of the auctioneers found they needed to imbibe during the evening, to keep their vocal cords lubricated, of course. Twinkling eyes would accompany a cry of 'Weigh up that lady's leg!' during a transaction. These late-evening auctions of meat at the weekend were an important part of the poorest families' livelihood. For a few bob, they could secure a joint of meat that would feed the entire family for a good part of the following week. Generally, the pattern was: Sunday, a roast dinner; Monday, cold meat with a fried vegetable hash, popularly known as 'bubble and squeak'; Tuesday, the remains of the joint as a nutritious 'stew-up' in the pot that was in near-constant use – the only means by which the family could economically be fed.

The sounds from the professional street entertainers, meanwhile, were as diverse as their audiences' lifestyles, and catered for two clearly-defined markets. First, the residents of the World's End neighbourhood were served by a variety of performers and musicians who could have been classed as 'non-highbrow'. These ranged from the idiosyncratic chap who balanced bicycles on his forehead and performed head-stands on milk bottles – he had many facial scars as evidence of his commitment to his art – to the male drag concert party that danced and sang to the accompaniment of the inevitable barrel organ. Their audiences would comprise the children sitting in the 'front stalls' – on the kerbstones and front house railings – and the older family members leaning from the upper windows, forming the 'circle' and 'balcony'. At the finale of the acts, it would only be 'ha'pennies from heaven' that rained down upon them because of the habitual shortage of cash.

All forms of the arts were represented and there was even one performer who sang his own compositions and recited his own verse, aimed largely at younger audiences. He was referred to as 'You Naughty Boy' as this was the opening line of his much-repeated principal recitation. He was able to keep his young patrons attentive during his act, which in itself was no mean achievement. While he was therefore regarded with affection and even admiration by the parents, he was still generally considered by them to be 'a bit touched'. This could be debatable, however, as more ha'pennies seemed to rain down on him than on his fellow artistes.

The second category of performers were the buskers who entertained the twice-nightly queues outside the two local music halls, the Chelsea Palace in the King's Road and the Granville Theatre in Walham Green, near the Chelsea Football Club ground, which was actually in the borough of Fulham. Standards of entertainment were high, both inside and outside the walls of these 'variety palaces'. Long before they were internationally known, artistes like Flanagan and Allen could be viewed from 'the gods' for a tanner.

With its flamboyant baroque frontage and sedate dome, the Chelsea Palace was regarded as offering a slightly more cerebral standard of entertainment, and I can remember being enraptured for the first time by the beauty of the ballet.[1] Outside, the queues were also kept absorbed by a high quality of performance by the buskers, which was surpassed only by their perfect timing. Two or three acts had to be squeezed into the short period during which the queue was formed, and, without fail, the last act completed its collection just as the tail-end disappeared through the narrow door leading to the pay-desk, pit and stalls. Not a penny was lost.

Some of these artistes looked as if they had performed in front of more critical audiences, particularly an accordionist who had shoulder-length grey hair, sported a bow-tie and velvet jacket, and sat on a bicycle saddle fitted to the end of a wooden pole. But the *élite* of the street musicians were those who played the prosperous thoroughfares of Chelsea, such as Cheyne Walk and the Royal Hospital Road, where the wealthy residents varied from the titled to the infamous. Two of the most memorable of these buskers were the harpist who pushed his cumbersome instrument on a hand-barrow to each roadside venue, and the pianist who transported his even more unwieldy and weighty instrument on a horse-drawn cart! Not for them reliance on 'ha'pennies from heaven', more the occasional half-crown and, now and again, even a ten-bob note.

As a young man, I spent many enjoyable hours with my

friends seated in the pit stalls of the Chelsea Palace enjoying the magical entertainment of performers of the calibre of Nellie Wallace, Hetty King and Harry Champion. I cannot remember ever being disappointed by a show. This, I must admit, was not always due to the prowess of the artistes, as some credit must go to the Bass 'Old Mild' served from barrels in the pit bar at the expensive price of sixpence per pint. This nectar had the capability of turning the most mediocre performance into a show-stopper!

Although he was not a busker, there was one final 'street performer' who managed to entertain most onlookers. The lamp-lighter carried out his duties as an employee of the local corporation in a highly competent and efficient manner. He would appear nightly, mounted on a bicycle, carrying in one hand a pole about 8 ft long, on top of which he was able, by some mysterious means, to produce a flame. He would approach each lamp-post in turn and, with fantastic dexterity, place the top of the pole through the bottom of the glass lamp, simultaneously operating the gas switch as the flame ignited the veritas mantle – the delicate asbestos filament inside the lamp. This complicated action was performed without dismounting from his cycle – and, indeed, while it still seemed to be in motion. His prowess over the years, although apparently taken for granted by his corporation employers, gained him admiration and respect, at least among us, the younger generation. I have always shared the romanticism of those who have paid tribute in song and verse to 'the old lamp-lighter of long ago'.

I am sure there were many hundreds more cries emanating from those back-streets. As these were cries for help and came from the heart, however, they were often inaudible and went unheeded.

Looking back at the era, when so much poverty was experienced by the hundreds of inhabitants compressed into that small area, I now realise that a life which was more than mere existence was possible, because adversity was mostly shared.

The near-communal lifestyle generated a bond of comradeship between us that conceivably could not have flourished in a more prosperous environment.

It was little more than a decade earlier that the residents of what was effectively a ghetto had experienced the trauma of the Great War, and now they were destined to suffer the ravages of what came to be known as the 'Hungry Thirties'. Few of the promises made to them by the politicians were honoured. It was this failure by the authorities to deliver on their wartime assurances that so infuriated the young Oswald Mosley, whose initially worthy invective against the evils of mass unemployment was soon to be insidiously sidetracked into that other evil of fascism. Like so many younger political activists of the time – including myself – he was frustrated by what he saw as the inertia of the old men in armchairs who ran the country, in the famous phrase, 'the hard-faced men who had done well out of the war'; they were failing woefully to adapt to the post-1918 economic and global conditions or to fulfil the pledges they had made about the new sort of social order that would be reconstructed from the devastation of the Western Front. Mosley saw himself as the champion of the wartime generation. The vast reservoir of disaffection among ordinary people at the inability of conventional, mainstream politics to respond to the crisis provided a fertile breeding ground for the fascist philosophy. It was no, surprise, therefore, that many working-class people, though misguided, rallied to the fascist cause.

As a socialist, of course, I recognise that people are the products of their backgrounds, their times and their circumstances. Just as I was shaped by the poverty but solidarity of the World's End, so Oswald Mosley was the product of what his son has tellingly described as 'a tendency ferocious and dismal which haunted people with too many servants and not enough to do'. In his case, though, this was combined with a streak of arrogance and self-belief, and a sense of his own destiny, that were to prove an inflammable formula.

Having been a combatant himself, Mosley believed that the nation owed more to its ex-servicemen than it was offering them. There was certainly no evidence of a 'land fit for heroes'. There was, however, an abundance of heroes if you looked for them, down every street and on every corner. Most were clearly identifiable by the fact that they had lost limbs, although others were not so obviously maimed – until their tell-tale coughs betrayed the havoc wreaked on their lungs by the mustard gas in the trenches. They still wore, with some pride, the silver-coloured 'Disabled Ex-Serviceman's Badge' in their lapels.[2]

Even so, from all the poverty and tragedy suffered during that era, there emerges an all-pervasive sense of the depth of camaraderie and humour that prevailed; it is particularly evident to fortunates like me who shared the experiences of those times. Indeed, it was these qualities, and the characters who exhibited them, that made our lives at all endurable.

NOTES

1 The Chelsea Palace was the work of the acclaimed theatre designer Frank Matcham, who was also responsible for the exquisite Grand Theatre in Blackpool (1894) – the stage of which has since seen appearances by such luminaries as the present Prime Minister's father-in-law, Tony Booth. During the 1996 Labour Party conference I had a pointed but light-hearted exchange with the actor about his son-in-law's policy on pensions! On the final day of the 1998 conference, he married for the fourth time, at the age of 66. It was his bride Stephanie Buckley's fifth wedding, and the couple had 11 children between them – one of whom was the Prime Minister's wife, Cherie. With Mr and Mrs Blair in attendance on their way home from Blackpool, the couple had their marriage blessed at a church in Walton, Merseyside.

Another Matcham masterpiece was the magnificent Empress Ballroom (1896) in Blackpool's Winter Gardens, an ebullient riot of gilt galleries, sumptuous chandeliers and imposing pillars, capped by a superb barrel-vaulted ceiling. As a steward, delegate or observer at successive party conferences, I have witnessed decades of political high drama in the huge but oddly intimate ballroom, with speeches by the likes of Bevan and Blair, Kinnock and Callaghan. So Frank Matcham contributed both to my theatrical and political awareness!

2   Mosley had himself been injured in the First World War in a flying accident, which exacerbated an earlier leg injury he had sustained in a fall from an upstairs window at Sandhurst. As a result, like my boxing coach Hoppy, he had one leg shorter than the other. Nicholas Mosley says his father had an ability to laugh at himself – but I doubt whether anyone dared give him a similarly disrespectful nickname.

14

EPILOGUE: FIVE YEARS ON

It was early 1941, Oswald Mosley had been detained in Brixton Prison under the Emergency Powers Act and Britain stood alone against the Nazis, bombarded nightly by the *Luftwaffe*'s Blitz. I was standing in the blackness of the entrance to Leicester Square Tube station, looking down at the rain falling on the emergency cables running alongside the kerb as they glistened in the winter moonlight. I was beginning to feel lonely: the rest of the passengers who had been ushered off the train with me, when the line ahead was abruptly closed, had mostly disappeared into the blackout, making their uncertain way to who-knows-where.

It was impossible to know whether it was an air raid or an all-clear as the boom of distant guns and the searchlight beams above were no guide: they were always present, anyway, after dark. I was feeling weary after a long and hazardous journey from my RAF camp in Lancashire to Euston station, the final couple of hours of which were spent at a snail's-pace, travelling through an air raid with burning buildings on both sides of the tracks.

I was contemplating how I was going to reach my destination in Chelsea when a War Reserve policeman emerged from the gloom of the street. I explained my problem to him, and could hardly believe it when he told me that, if I stood on the corner of the street a hundred yards from the Tube station, a bus would eventually arrive that would take me somewhere in the direction I needed, on its way to south London via a bridge across the Thames. That was despite an air raid alert which he assured me was in progress at the time!

I stood in a doorway awaiting the improbable bus and,

despite the distant guns and the occasional swish of a passing ARP (Air Raid Precautions) vehicle, I felt alone, in an unreal world. My reverie was rudely but gratefully interrupted after about ten minutes by the sudden appearance round the corner, ghost-like, of the bus, with the glow from the slits of its hooded headlamp grille just discernible.

The bus jerked to a stop and, as no-one got off, I jumped on to the rear platform; immediately it pulled away, to continue what seemed like a phantom journey. The lower deck appeared fairly crowded, but I wasn't aware of the presence of a conductor as no fares were being collected, which would have been impossible in the darkness in any case. I swayed to-and-fro on the platform as the vehicle jolted along at an incredible speed, considering the visibility for the driver (an unsung working-class hero if ever there was one). It was impossible to hold a conversation with any of the denizens of the darkened lower deck, so, knowing the bus was to cross the river eventually, I decided to stay on the platform until I could see the bridge and to jump off before it continued its journey to south London.

Soon I realised that we were in the Victoria area of the Vauxhall Bridge Road. Assuming the bus would shortly be crossing the Vauxhall Bridge, I took the opportunity to leap off as the vehicle slowed down near Victoria Station – to the welcome accompaniment of an all-clear siren. Walking past the formidable façade of the Southern Railway's great terminus in the early hours, I realised that I would have to complete the final stage of my journey on foot. After my experiences since I had set off from Lancashire the previous morning, however, this seemed like child's play, and I made my way through the streets of Pimlico into Sloane Square, the gateway to Chelsea.

As I walked across the square into the King's Road, I was angry at seeing, for the first time, the destruction of an area for which I had such affection. Glass from Peter Jones, the department store, was strewn across the pavements and the road. I found myself feeling for windows in the frontages of the small, select shops opposite, but they were not there.

Continuing past the Duke of York's Territorial head-quarters, which evoked many memories of my schoolboy boxing days, I walked on to the Black House, Mosley's former fascist base. I felt no satisfaction at seeing its battered frontage and now-dilapidated appearance; just an anger that Mosley's mentors had succeeded – where he had failed – in reducing the King's Road and its surroundings to such a state of destruction. The fascists of Germany had done what the home-grown variety had failed to do, when we had defeated the BUF and its foul aspirations. There was also the piquancy of the fact that his former headquarters had been devastated by those whose political philosophy he shared. Such was the confidence, even in those desperate times, that the enemy would be defeated that I never imagined that his Nazi friends might be able to restore him in triumph as a fascist dictator of Britain.

Dawn was breaking as I continued westward along the road and, as the day grew lighter and the streets began to fill with people and vehicles, it became more evident that the area had suffered badly that night. Reaching the World's End, I found many families gathered in the square and around the St John's Mission; ropes had been placed across the King's Road and the area leading down to the river, barring access. St John's Church had been destroyed by a bomb the year before, but services continued in the mission hall.

I soon learned that an unexploded landmine had been dropped in Uverdale Road, and that a mass evacuation of the residents had taken place, many of them being housed in the bomb-battered hall. By now, I was really alarmed, as those evacuated would have included my wife and our baby, with the rest of the family; they lived in that street and, of course, spent the nights in the air-raid shelters with all their neighbours.

Frantic inquiries soon established that Dolly and the family had not been evacuated to the mission hall but instead had made their way to nearby Fulham. This was where Dolly and I still rented a one-bedroom flat, with difficulty – the price was 12s/6d a week, including an air-raid shelter! I trudged (wearily

105

by now) to Fulham to be re-united with my family. I had used half of the allotted 48 hours of my pass to get there, but this was forgotten in the joy of seeing my loved ones safe and unharmed.

Although the events of that weekend were but a minute microcosm of what happened across the globe in those six terrible years, they are etched ineradicably in my memory. It was then that I witnessed my beloved King's Road and World's End, and their people, suffering so grievously from the fascism that we – its former 'street-urchins' – had long recognised and hated. Of course, a quarter of a century later, the King's Road was to dust itself down and swing once more. With its trendy stores and boutiques, it was to become the most vibrant symbol of 'Swinging London' under Harold Wilson's 1964 and 1966 Labour Governments. And, a further 30 years on, Tony Blair's New Labour was to rebrand the capital as the emblem of 'Cool Britannia' – which just proves that, in politics, *plus ça change*. But that, again, is another story.